INDUSTRIALISM INUSTRIAL DEMOCRACY & WORLD GOVERNANCE

TILAHUN TASSEW

©Tilahun Tassew 2013

Forward your comments and questions to the author using the following addresses. tilahuntassew@yahoo.com or tilahuntassew7@gmail.com; P.O.Box 1110/1033, Addis Ababa, Ethiopia.

ISBN-13:978-1491069301

ISBN-10: 1491069309

Title ID: 4373109

Published in USA

Authors page:
https://www.amazon.com/author/ethiopiannovelist

Publishing history
First published on Create Space Amazon July 2003
Second edition September 2003

CONTENTS

Acronyms...4

PREFACE..5

INTRODUCTION 13

1. INTRODUCING THE DEMOCRATIC PERSPECTIVE IN DEVELOPMENT STUDIES..20

2. THE DEMOCRATIC PERSPECTIVE IN DEVELOPMENT STUDIES AS A THEORETICAL APPROACH..................48

3. RELEVANCE OF THE DEMOCRATIC PERSPECTIVE IN DEVELOPMENT STUDIES..85

4. THE DEMOCRATIC PERSPECTIVE IN DEVELOPMENT STUDIES AS A POLICY IMPERATIVE..116

SUMMARY 134

Postscript..141

REFERENCES..150

In love to my grandchildren Elizabeth, Caleb and Iyoab

Acronyms

DPDS Democratic Perspective in Development Studies
ISI   Import Substitution Industrialization
ELI   Export Led Industrialization
GSA   General Structural Adjustment
SAP   Structural Adjustment Program

PREFACE

Not long ago, I came across a thesis I wrote in partial fulfillment of Masters of Arts in development studies. The thesis was sent to me from my alma mater, the Institute of Social Studies in The Hague, The Netherlands. I went through it and found it intriguing and even helpful to explain the current world financial crisis. I think most who ever got the chance to reread their thesis after long years will experience similar feelings. My thesis was written during the collapse of the Soviet Union after Gorbachev created the illusion that the socialist system would compromise with liberalist economic, social and political systems. It was hoped that the west might take reciprocal measures and lead to a world governance based on universal justice, standardization and internationalism. A new world order where national chauvinism relegated seemed a possible outcome.

It was not long when things began to wobble as was in the aftermath of the Second World War. The end of the Second World War was expected to usher in a world governance with the convergence of the two

European traditions namely, socialism and liberalism.

A world empire with U.S as a sole owner of the atomic bomb and the Baruch Plan for peace with U.S dominance was pushed, but failed to be realized. Rather the

Second World War ended in a bipolar world which continued the Second World War by what was named the "Cold War", between the two ideological fronts of socialism and liberalism, with the rest of the countries allied beside the two powers USSR and USA.

The idea about a league of sovereign states like the UN to lead to a world government was flawed. With the emergence of the bipolar world, the flaw in the UN structure was vivid in Sir David Low's cartoon of November 8, 1945, where a chair for five big persons symbolized the Security Council. The three chairs were already occupied and the two were vacant waiting for an occupant, it seemed reserved for Russia and its ally.

The world lost another chance of democratic world governance at the end of the Cold War in what seemed similar paths. The same flawed logic about a chair for 20 big persons while the five is already occupied is being entertained for the United Nations Security Council.

"I'm Here To Stay, Too"

In the aftermath of the Cold War, the nation state seemed not to give way to world governance but flourished and got strengthened. Eritrea was separated from Ethiopia, Yugoslavia disintegrated into its components nation states and South Sudan was born separated from The Sudan. The former Soviet Union emerged as new states.

The aftermath of the Second World War and the Cold War concretized as in a similar fashion. David Low's cartoon of the time where a League of Nation, which died of lack of exercise, looks at the armed UN carried away by USA seemed current if we delete the tombstone along with the League of Nations.

I wrote my thesis in the era of Gorbachev with full confidence about democratization of work place and larger societies in a world government where socialism and liberalism converged. The thesis forwarded a new development paradigm for the underdeveloped world in light of the convergence of liberalism and socialism. A year has not passed before this dream was shattered. But I entertain this view now and forever.

My interest to write this preface and publish my thesis, I received from my alma mater, strengthened when I read the thesis as if it is a paper written by somebody else. Most of you must have shared similar experience when reread your thesis wrote two or three decades earlier.

I reread the thesis in a different environment of the world economy than it was two decades earlier when it was written. In the first decade of the 21st century the world was engulfed in financial crisis. In Europe and USA the increasing role of the state brought back the need for the rational of the two traditions of liberalism and socialism as components which should converge.

Of course, the 21st century also showed the need for triangulation of the Chinese Confucian tradition of peace and beauty with the two European traditions. African family values might also be a fourth dimension. The Arabs religious fervor the fifth one.

The convergence of the two European traditions has been flawed in the aftermaths of the Second World War and the conclusion of the Cold War era. A New Cold War looms in the horizon. Russia, China and other powers might move to the Mediterranean and Pacific world to protect their national interests and USA might try to defend its holdings with unmanned aircraft and technological superiority. The last soldiers of the nation state may be technological entities or robots. On the other hand knowledge is becoming universal and the edge in technology is becoming irrelevant. The world seems to be in greater danger than it was during the Cold War. The New Cold War seemed to take forms in what we see in Libya, Egypt and Syria. As it was during colonialism so also now the victims are the developing world and the peripheries of the developed countries. It is different from the proxy war fields of the Cold War era only in the means it uses not in its destructive nature.

The destructiveness of the New Cold War (NCW) could be witnessed in Libya, Egypt, Yemen, Syria, Afghanistan, and Somalia. It might engulf Africa, Asia, Arabian Peninsula and the peripheries of the developed world. National states are fragmented into fifes and kingdoms, national armies into chieftains armed with modern weapon, modernism with traditional and religious fanaticism

Through passing in such an inferno the world at last may learn to compromise with itself in world governance based on laws, standards, world parliament, courts and strengthened UN Security and Economic Councils. USA has a great role to play in this process. It has to start from the scratch and bring the convergence of the two European traditions through compromise and discussion and not through Baruch Plan. This requires a world where peace and tranquility are dominant with an economic advancement that is possible through reconstruction and construction of the infrastructure of Africa, Asia, Latin America and the renewal of the infrastructures in the developed world and the discouragement of upheavals for democracy or plutocracy. During colonialism and what other called the Industrial Revolution the emphasis was on application of science and technology to industry and agriculture, clearing of whole continents for cultivation, canalization of rivers and the modern age should focus on infrastructure building and renewal that has never been witnessed in its width and breadth. Every revolution of significance should unfetter the productive forces and this will be the challenge for the 21st century.

The paper that dealt with work place democratization through applying the merger of the two traditions seemed still relevant to me. Thus, I decided to publish it as a book. If ever you come by this book, I think the idea will find an ear which is the process for dissemination, realization and concretization of ideas into realities.

The thesis was given a long title as follows: The Democratic Perspective: A Preliminary Theory about Industrialism and Industrial Democracy (A Contribution to Development Studies). I found out the title has to be shorter and thus it was published with a new title which in essence is a summary of the lengthy one dropped. While rereading the thesis I made editorial corrections otherwise I left it as it was before.

    I understood that the book does not only need preface but also a postscript which I annexed at the end of the book. The postscript updated my dream, which has never been static but rousing. That is what is known as a good dream. I think we should be dreamers of the future where our descendants dwell and prosper or God forbid, perish in a post New Cold War. Every individual has to respond to the challenge in an accountable way.

July 2013.

INTRODUCTION

"Ritz-Carlton Theory. This theory attributed to the notable U.S strategist William Kaufmann says that if a Soviet strategic analyst was marooned in a Boston hotel room with only U.S journals such as ORBIS and STRATEGIC REVIEW to read, then he would form an opinion about U.S intentions as prejudiced as the view held by some Western analysts of Soviet intentions derived from reading Soviet military and strategic journals."

Michael Sheehan & H Wyllie 1986:210

Development study, about the developing world, has been invariably taken as appendage of theories forwarded to understand the stages of capitalist society. If a lesson is to be derived from the history of capitalist society that is useful to the developing world, the industrial (capitalist) society must be scrutinized from its unique features that make it different from hitherto societies, and that allowed it to dramatically change the productive forces outside "the discovery of gold and silver in America, the extirpation, enslavement and entombment in mines of the aboriginal population, the beginning of the conquest and looting of the East Indies, the turning of Africa into a warren for the commercial hunting of black-skins .. "(Marx, Karl, 1974:703-4); the protestant ethic and spirit of capitalism (Weber); the accumulation of capital and prerequisites for take offs (Rostow and Gerschenkron); and most of all the idea that capital needed for further development is generated by extraction of surplus from labor power.

This paper, by basing the productivity and sustainable growth of industrial society in a unique type of management and trade union relationship at the enterprise level, and the two traditions of liberalism and socialism, at the larger society level, forwards a development theory. In industrial society although not in developing societies as interest representation in the enterprise is based on the twin grounds of productivity (interest of the management) and social justice (that of trade unions); we have now a socio-economic system, for the first time in history, whereby the political structure and economic growth of the industrial society are its concomitant basic identifying features. This paper by taking the assumption that technological innovation and surplus for further capital formation come from the competitive nature of enterprises within the setting of the above relations in the competing enterprises raises trade union management relationship into a theorizing point for development studies.

This paper, by taking this aspect and by a method of abstraction, attempts to show the working of the industrial society, and its driving force of sustainable and fast development, by way of a new theoretical perspective[1]. It also applying the same perspective to a cross-cultural study in the developing world situation, attempts to develop models for promoting industrialization and the advancement of a realistic system of industrial relation in the so called Third World .

Thus, the various perspectives on capitalist development, industrialization,

---

[1] The Manifesto put the development thrust of the industrial society as follows: "The bourgeoisie, during its rule of scarce one hundred years, has created more massive and more colossal productive forces than have all preceding generations together. Subjection of nature's forces to man, machinery, application of Chemistry to industry and agriculture, steam-navigation, railways, electric telegraphs, clearing of whole continents for cultivation, canalization of rivers. whole populations conjured out of the ground - what earlier century had even a presentiment that such productive forces slumbered in the lap of social labor?

industrialism, and industrial relations will be scrutinized from the point of view of developmental issues. As the Reformation, the Enlightenment, the Industrialization process and even the history of tribal and traditional societies interested Marx and Weber in proving their theories, the historian of science may see in each of them advancement in mathematics, natural and social sciences. A student of development studies, concerned about the developing world, on the other hand, may read the past events in light of searching a lesson for industrialization. While the facts are the same, a development student will read them differently. So must be reread the life and time of Marx, Weber and other development theoreticians.[2]

Other than simulating the Marxian and Weberian perspectives by proxy,[3] it should

---

[2] Thus, Marx as the great thinker is useful when critically analyzed. Marxism was debased into industrialization for political power and national strife and civil war during the Cold War. Weber as a theoretician and alternative can be criticized but he was also debased for ideological struggle during the Cold War.

[3] J Gerschenkron rightly observes that our understanding of industrialization is highly influenced by grand Marxian generalization (Gerschenkron: 1979:6). So also with the rise of interest in underdeveloped countries interest in Weberian economic sociology was revived (Spiegel 1971:430).

be noted that the cold war had a profound effect on development studies about the third world as it had to become an appendage of the struggle of the "two systems". The Russian revolutionary, Bukharin foresaw the emergence of two world markets: one socialist and the other capitalist. He argued the need for integrating the backward countries with the socialist world market an idea that became a contesting issue not only in the realm of politics but also in the post-World War II development theorizing. With the commencement of the cold war, and with the third world countries getting their independence, there was a struggle between the capitalist and the socialist block, to widen their respective spheres of influence. It is the implication of the points outlined above on development studies that should suggest reassessment of existing development theories as they are directed to the third world, and the importance of such study for development purpose.

Finally, some words on the scope and structure of the paper. The aim of this paper is to forward a "new theoretical perspective", in order to better understand industrialism, industrialization, industrial relations and industrial democracy, for the sole purpose of contributing to development studies for the third world. Thus, the development of the capitalist society with its stages in the industrialized countries is not the subject matter here. The term development study has to be understood in this paper as referring to the development of the underdeveloped countries when otherwise not specified.

Chapter 1 is a historical approach in which the different approaches will be examined; they will be scrutinized based on their significance to developmental studies and understanding the industrial society, to derive appropriate lessons to the developing world. The hitherto perspectives are summarized as conspiratorial or pessimistic perspectives and the new perspective, the democratic Perspective in Development Studies (DPDS), which this paper opts for, is introduced.

In chapter 2, the DPDS will be expounded as a new theoretical approach to understand industrialism, industrial relations and industrial democracy. Some models will be drawn and evidence of their viability is presented.

In chapter 3, the DPDS will be used to analyze the related problems in the underdeveloped world. The difference, in terms of the enterprise and, motive of industrial production, between the industrial society and the underdeveloped world will be examined, along with the larger society of the underdeveloped world. Models will be developed and verifications presented. What should be changed in the underdeveloped world to bring about industrialism will also be discussed.

Chapter 4 deals with the DPDS as a policy imperative, taking a hypothetical third world country adopting the DPDS as a policy imperative, its impacts on social, political and economic fabric, as well as on the different classes and groups of the hypothetical society will be simulated. The DPDS, is conceived, neither from stubbornness, (arising from negating hitherto unworkable methods) nor skepticism, (from a belief that theories propounded to understand the stages of capitalist society are not useful for the third world which is still backward) even though these are not out of place. Development studies beg for such general theory to be put forward to be tested in the fire of criticism, to reach to a qualitative perspective, which is viable and handy.

1. INTRODUCING THE DEMOCRATIC PERSPECTIVE IN DEVELOPMENT STUDIES

"As always, the first prerequisite for changing a situation in a desired direction is to understand it." Alan Fox

Development studies are based on implications of the understanding of the industrial society. This is because industrialization is a goal by itself[4]. The history of the development of the industrial society and theories forwarded to understand it has a great impact on the model the proponents of developmental studies suggest for the third world[5]. Thus, the reexamination

---

[4] The concept of development as a flawed concept and a polemical issue in every day discussion takes the medieval form of ecclesiastical sophistry of how many angels could stand on a tip of a needle. People get inclined to assert about the type of the industrialization: industrialization with a human face or not before answering in a tangible way how industrialization could be achieved. In the DPDS state socialism is taken mainly as an industrialization strategy that was adopted after the 1917 revolution. In the present age, the underdeveloped world has to find its own way for development and/or industrialization.

[5] The Rostow and Gerschenkron models are cases in point.

and refinement or change of the general theories about industrial society is of paramount importance.

1.1 The flawed concept of development studies

For whatever they amount in viability there were forwarded axioms abut the driving force of the capitalist system in its capacity of increasing productivity and the expansion of its material wealth. The entrepreneur was taken as its driving force. So too the market was considered. Labor as the producer was put as a counter point. Greed and personal enrichment motive was not forgotten. Plunder and thievery were not excluded. Nor spirit, form and technique[6] were ignored.

---

[6] Werner Sombert (1863 -1941) developed a conceptual scheme to explore the morphology, or structure, of different economic systems, classifying them by their "spirit ,"their "form," and their "technique". Thus he would characterize the spirit of capitalism as dominated by the ideas of acquisition, competition, and rationality; its form as a free, decentralized, market oriented private enterprise system; and its technology as ever changing and geared to advances in productivity (Spiegel H.W, 1971:428). S. Marglin (1984: 148-9) on the other hand considers that division of labor was promoted more by the need to control rather than efficiency.

Karl Marx and Max Weber but have a special significance. It doesn't seem that there is much that development study directed to the under developed countries, could adopt directly from Marx and Weber analysis of the genesis of capitalism as neo- Marxian and Neo-Weberian try to do. Neither does it seem that the justification for socialist oriented and capitalist oriented forms of development imposed because of power block politicking during the Cold War have direct justification in Marx and Weber.

Marx was primarily interested to show the exploitative nature of the capitalist system and that this system is destined to become a fetter to production and thus it will be overthrown[7].' Nor does the study about capitalism, industrial society, as propounded by Marx seem to emphasis what will happen to the backward countries in the event of the full development of capitalism and the revolution to socialism in the advanced capitalist countries. This question was confronted in

---

[7] That Marx's primary interest was to prove the inevitability of socialism is commented by many. "In its broad outline, Marx's doctrine was but another variant of German historicism, a theory of economic stages or periods which invoked in order to assert, not the peculiar character of the German economy as other historical economists had done but the inevitability of socialism" (SPiegel:457).

earnest after the Second World War when most colonies gained their independence and the capitalist and non-capitalist ways for development became important in the relation between the Soviet Union and United States camps.

The earlier study of Bukharin about the international division of labor and the emergence of two world markets and the need to integrate the backward countries into the socialist world market is a case in point. Bukharin's study about the world market and the need of integrating the back ward economies into the socialist world market prior to the Second World War was motivated by the exclusion of the Soviet Union from the world market. Thus, he saw the tactical importance of the emergence of two world markets, namely, the socialist world market and the capitalist world market.

For Marx, development in the restricted sense of capitalist creation of wealth can be described in a twofold manner. In its material content, development is about the expansion of productive forces and the increased production of commodities. In its form, development is about the accumulation of capital. That is to say, the drive of capital both to appropriate the surplus-value produced by labor and embodied in the commodities and to realize it by selling the commodities in the market, thus allowing the process to be repeated on a wider scale"(Larrain, Jorge,1989:41). Thus, the neo-Marxists sophistication arises from another direction. The neo-Marxists use Marx's thesis on historical materialism in proxy to adopt it to development studies. Here thus it was the transition from one mode of production to another say from feudalism to capitalism was taken to be development thus to transform forcefully the production relations was assumed to end up in bringing development. That is to say creation of a prerequisite for capitalist development. The same was thought about jumping the stage of capitalism into socialism: Building the material basis of socialism – its prerequisite.

Max Weber contributed not to economics proper but to economic sociology. "Weber's investigation of the protestant origin of capitalism falls into this range of work, as do his explorations of the socioeconomic impact of the great religions. This type of approach has assumed a new significance with the current concern about underdeveloped countries (Spiegel, 1971: 430). Thus so too Weber was not directly interested in the impetus of the capitalist society except its origin and the rationalization of its continuity in a covered up debate with Marx[8].

Max Weber shares many things with Marx. Like Marx, he sought an integration of structure, culture and social interests in historical explanation and insisted on historical specificity. Like Marx, he has made social power and class relation central to his understanding of society but gave credence to the roles of actors and the theories of rationalization and bureaucratic organizations[9].

---

[8] H Gerth and D Martindale in their preface to the translation of Weber wrote as follows: "Weber stood between the two towering critics of modern western culture, Marx and Nietzsche, dealing simultaneously with Marx' attacks on the world of capitalism as irrational "wage slavery" and "anarchy of production," in which is compelled to alienate the truly human, and with Nietzsche's attacks on democracy and Christianity, on rational and ethical universalism (Gerth, H & Martindale, D 1952:xi-xii).

[9] The distinction between Marx and Weber is summarized by Burris (1987:68) as follows: Marx takes class relations as paramount Weber sees class outweighed by non-class forms of associations. Weber thought domination is an end by itself, while Marx thought class relation and class conflict is exploitative. For Marx classes are results of social relations of production while for Weber they are common positions within the market.

But Marx and Weber are the result of their times. To understand the development in thought from the enlightenment to Edmund Burke and Hegel and then to Darwin and Marx and Marx to Weber we have to reexamine the interpretation of history because historical mindedness was the core of their thinking which differentiates them from the enlightenment era. Secondly, since they are human beings "There is a moral and religious as well as a material environment which sets its stamp on the individual, even when he is least conscious of it" (Tawney R.H 1960: 12).

Let's start with Marx. The British Health and Morals Act and the first legislation for the protection of the young in Zurich were legislated 16 years and one year, respectively, before Marx was born. When Marx was 16 years old the legislation that outlaws formation of trade unions was repealed in the United Kingdom in 1824 for the first time and it was still in force in France when Marx died. When he was 30, the Swiss Canton enacted the first legislation limiting the working hours of adults. Two years before his death the hours of work of children to nine hours per day and of adults to ten per day was enacted in India. Sickness insurance and workmen's compensation were pioneered by Germany when Marx was dying in 1883 and 1884. New Zealand pioneered compulsory arbitration in industrial dispute in the 1890s almost a decade after Marx was deceased.

Thus, what Marx observed at the time was the struggle of the working class without a legal trade union upholding social and economic justice. The state he witnessed as the instrument of the propertied class. It was natural to see thus in the working class the seed of the future.

Max Weber became politically active in the left liberal Protestant Social Union (Evangelist-Soziale Verein) almost a decade after Marx's death in the 1890s and in his opinion the working class was not ready to accept the responsibilities of power and forwarded the idea that the nation as a whole should mature by a conscious policy of overseas imperial expansion. He advanced an ideology known as "liberal imperialism"(E.B. Vol. 19: 715). Weber by confronting Marx created "a methodology and a body of literature dealing with the sociology of religion, the sociology of political parties, small group behavior, and the philosophy of history "(EB. Vol. 19: 716). Weber died 4 years after witnessing the October Revolution of 1917 arguing political sobriety in his country after helping in the founding of the German Democratic Party and the drafting of the new constitution.

The above points were raised not as a critique of Marx and Weber analysis of the genesis of capitalism but only to show that the main thrust of their research was on the stages of capitalist development and not how to industrialize the backward countries and that development study has to start from afresh. What is directly important for this paper is the development in the study of the relationship between management and trade unions, which this paper uses as basis for theorizing for development studies[10].

The Ricardian socialists before Marx, (Charles Hall 1740-1820, William Thompson 1775-1883, Thomas Hodgskin 1787-1869, John Gray 1797-1883) are the ones who tried to relate the theory of surplus value to the secure proper functioning of the economy. The Ricardian socialists saw the concomitant existence of productivity and social justice as necessary to the industrial society. From the labor theory of value they derived theories of exploitation and surplus value "arguing that

---

[10] The rise of development studies in an atmosphere of the Cold War revived the Weberian approaches in the West. Developmental study tried to reach a general theoretical scheme from the economic and social anthropological history of the advanced countries. The problem of comparability and its failure led it to consider cultural variables and threw it into the lap of social anthropology. (Hoselitz. Bert F. 1952: v-vii).

the wage system deprived the laborer of the value of the whole product of his industry. To replenish this share was to them a requirement of justice as well as a means to secure the proper functioning of the economy. For the achievement of these ends they proposed to rely on cooperative organizations, the trade union movement, and monetary reform"(Spiegel: 442). The Ricardian socialists had identified the sustainability embedded in the industrial society.

The attempt to identify the mechanism of the industrial society that enables it to function normally is an important issue especially for the present day development studies. The Ricardian socialists view was not directed to contribute to development studies. However, the rise of industrial relation in the 1940s, focusing primarily on management-trade union relationship has much impact on this paper for forwarding a development theory.

Industrial relations as a field emerged from economics by making a distinction of roles. J Dunlop (1985:382-3) makes the distinction as follow: "Economics centers its attention on the national product (output) and its variations over time, and industrial relations centers its attention on the rules of the system and their variations over time." Thus interest in the importance of the trade union management relations got its momentum in the academic world. However, this relationship between management and trade unions was not put to use as a starting point for development studies, which this paper is opting to do now.

When industrial relations emerged as a distinctive field in the 1940s and 1950s much was changed from the time of Marx and Weber. When Kerr et al. wrote Industrialism and Industrial Man and J.k Galbraith, The New industrial State respectively in 1960 and 1967 the terms management and managers have developed with the development of large corporations being run not by owners but with those who have no appreciable share in the capital of the enterprise. Trade union membership has gone down in relation to rising employment. The relation of the state to the economy in U.S and Europe was exceeding avowed socialist states like India (Galbraith J. K 1967:2).

When Clark Kerr and John T. Dunlop were 24 and 21 years old, respectively labor relations act was passed in USA and when they were 33 and 36 another act on the same line was added. When their Industrialism and Industrial Man was first published in 1960 Khrushchev's secret speech and the Czechoslovakian apprising had unveiled the vulnerability of the state socialist system.

Kerr et al. shortcoming was to think that the uniformity of the technological base will create a momentum to industrialization and thus to industrialism and will give rise to similar if not identical industrial relations system. The ideas of the 19th-century concept of progress had crept in their study's conclusion about industrialization. This has been the fate of current comparative studies of "modernization" and industrialization (E.B Vol. 16:921). Kerr et al. general theory too concentrated too much on the role of the elite. The institutionalization of conflict and the Weberian motive of actors and the concept of class even though it was declared free from the syndrome of the debate with Marx.

So Kerr et al. industrial relation system was highly influenced by Max Weber analysis of human action in terms of the motive of the actors on one hand and on the other the role of the state as an umpire of management and trade unions that was being reflected in the growing activities of the state and the growing role of management and technology at the time. The growing role of the state in their societies led them to see the state as one of the actors and technology and the growing role of management led them to see as management holding the seed of the future technology and the industrial economy the causal primacy.

The need for using management-trade union relationship as a starting point of development study was late to come but adumbration of its recognition were being seen here and there. for example Blumberg (1968:ch.5) was nearer to come to the recognition that a unique form of management trade unions relationship will result in increased workers productivity if not to general development of the productive forces. This paper by basing the productivity and sustainable growth of industrial society in a unique type of management and trade union relationships at the enterprise level and the concomitant existence of socialist and liberalist ideologies, according to the initial meaning of the terms, in the larger society, forwards a development theory appropriate for the LDCs.

Here hitherto approaches are made to a typology as follows based on three perspectives and seven assumptions heuristically to facilitate the argument for such an endeavor:

1.1.1 The conspiratorial perspective

Assumption # 1: The relationship between management and labor is a class struggle and it could end only in the abolition of capital.

Assumption # 2: Even though the relationship between labor and management are conflictual, conflict could be institutionalized and labor ameliorated

Assumption # 3: workers participatory schemes could be used for transforming capitalism into socialism.

1.1.2 The pessimistic perspective

Assumption # 4: Trade unions are no more important for management view and they could be laid off[11]

Assumption # 5 Trade unions have outlived their time and they have to join the mainstream of social movements.

1.1.3 The Democratic Perspective in Development Studies

(The idea this paper argues)

Assumption # 6: The democratic traditions and the viable growth of industrial society are embedded in its basic unit, the enterprise where management upheld order and productivity and trade unions equity and egalitarianism. Democratic society, democratization of work place is unthinkable without interest representation manifested in the enterprise and it could be positively

---

[11] This issue is discussed by Barbash (Barbash J 1990:117).

motivated only from accepting the basic structure.

Assumption #7: The less developed countries will reach industrialism when they build industrial society through transforming the relation of management and trade unions and this transformation is manifested in liberalism and socialism upheld by different groups in the larger society. This will require extensive general structural adjustment.

1.2 Concepts and terms

1.2.1 The Democratic Perspective in Development Studies as a paradigm for Developing Countries

The DPDS, when it takes the two categories of management and trade unions in development studies it does so by considering what each of them stand for as interest representatives of their institutions within the enterprise. Even when it analyzes the relationship of the enterprise to the larger society, it analyzes the larger society as interest representation of social classes as liberalism and socialism. The process where groups and social classes advance their interest in a concomitant conflict and cooperation atmosphere is called a democratic system. But when it is applied in the model construction here, its meaning is made to add economic momentum and thus it needs a definition as the concept of the DPDS.

1.2.2 Interest representation as a development momentum

Interest representation herein used has a different conceptual meaning than its day-to-day use. Here interest representation has not only political and social but also developmental momentum. Economic development momentum is a factor of growing productivity along social and political momentum.

The economic momentum may be derivative of the effect and cause. Take workers interest representation in an enterprise. Here the vehicle is the trade union and it stands for equity and egalitarianism in opposition to the productivity and order which management is interested in.

The economic momentum is thus said to be present when the interest of the workers in equity and egalitarianism finds expression, for example, in the demand for increased wages, which can only be fulfilled with the rise in productivity which management is interested in. Thus, what seems antagonistic in essence holds the key to advancement.

Interest representation of a political or social nature which does not fulfill the advancement of productivity as an economic interest is not taken here as an interest representation of a basic importance but a secondary one. It is taken as an aberration, which is not characteristic of the industrial society, which may be a phenomenon of its initial stage or misfit of its nature. In a situation where the interest of workers represented in a trade union and achieves rise in wages not from productivity rise but at the expense of farmers and peasants, which will be discussed in chapter 3, is said here to have no economic momentum and it is mostly found in third world or similar situations.

Interest representation as a concept adopted here is the unique feature of the industrial society. Thus, here for the first time in history we have a system where its political structure and economic growth is concomitantly its identifying and basic feature. At the enterprise level, the interest of trade unions in equity and egalitarianism cannot be fulfilled without the fulfillment of productivity and order that management upheld. The failure of the classical writers who doubted the ability of the system to generate a demand strong enough to absorb the output of the economy and the Marxian prediction that the proletariat will grow poorer arose from misunderstanding this basic phenomenon. The first were astounded with the capacity of the industrial society to produce the later with the misery of the working class at his time. In the third world, at present the ignorance of the above fact makes possible the justification of low wages. Interest representation brings out productivity and social justice as conscious goals of different interests and institutionalizes them. At the larger society level socialism and liberalism, become traditions. Thus in the enterprise we have trade unions interest and management interest as two categories and in the larger society level liberalism and socialism as two categories.

1.2.3 The Enterprise as a nucleus of Growth

The relationship between management and labor as a relationship between two interest representatives in the enterprise is a due process of democratization of society where management stands for productivity and order and trade Unions for equity and egalitarianism in a contextual process of cooperation and conflict[12].

---

[12] In the absence of such recognition it is surprisingly interesting that in France those who contributed much to the spread of capitalism are socialist oriented personalities. Alexander Gersthenkron (1952: 22) observes about French industrialization under Napoleon. III: "A large proportion of the men who reached positions of economic and financial influence upon Napoleon's advent to power were not isolated individuals. They belonged to a rather well-defined group. They were not Bonapartists but Saint Simonian Socialists.

Productivity & order 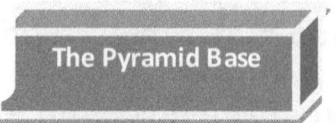 Equity &egalitarianism

These two categories are important in studying the industrial society. Other approaches with the flavor of two categories were used for different purposes. The purpose must be the point of departure. The enterprise as an organization can be looked as a system by simply considering the outside stimuli (inputs) and the associated responses (outputs), or for the purpose of affecting the organization within so as to improve its operations "as multi-level structure in a systems theoretic model of an organization" (Mesarovic M.D, Macko D.R & Tahahara Y, 1970:16) another approach of the same type is game theory. The emphasis is on the bargaining process within the organization disregarding the hierarchical structure. So is the theory of teams (ibid: 19). But here the two categories of productivity and order management upheld and equity and egalitarianism trade union s upheld could serve to analyze the development impetus of the unit of production in industrial society to use it in development study.

Collective bargaining in the last century has shown the validity of the generalization that management stands for productivity and order and trade unions for equity and egalitarianism in industrial society (in developing societies this might not be the case as will be shown later). Here thus, in the industrial society,[13] the bargaining process and aims is what shows that productivity and order are management motives and equity and egalitarianism of the trade union. This could be proved rationally and empirically[14]. But as will be shown later on what is considered management prerogative and trade union prerogative changes in time series in development. Trade union may assume what

---

[13] Here the defining term, industrial society, should be emphasized. In the DPDS such motives are only characteristic of the enterprise in the industrial society. Chapter 3 deals with the difference between the industrial society and the industrializing society and the motives of the management and trade unions. This difference is the basis for the paper's the6tizing on developmental imperatives.

[14] Descartes, Leibniz and Spinoza are well known in further developing the rational approach while Bacon, Locke, Hume and Newton are well known personalities arguing for a more empirical methodology. "Through the centuries, research and philosophical patterns of thinking have swung from one kind of emphasis to the other, and even today we can only prescribe balance without suggesting exactly how it can be achieved"(Hough, Louis 1970:18). This paper opts both approaches one or the other as it fits its aim.

were once management prerogatives of productivity and order and management shares what were once the equity and social justice prerogatives of trade unions. This is done by examining the history of trade union and management motives in the industrialized countries and current collective bargaining outcomes. In the history of trade unions, trade unions were standing for improved wages, working conditions, as well as for social justice outside the enterprise. Management from laissez-faire attitude grew up to paternalistic relations and then to social interest in the company towns and in international issues. While this has been well accepted and clear what researchers were not able to observe was that trade unions as they stand for equity and egalitarianism during their relation to management were fulfilling what are considered as management prerogatives of productivity and order. This process is not always harmonious as we have known in history sometimes it takes the form of conflict induced from either the management or the trade unions side.

1.2.4 Liberalism and Socialism

The relationship in the enterprise is evidenced in the larger society by the two great traditions of socialism and liberalism. In the larger society socialism and liberalism as the two great traditions and characteristics of industrial society emerge as reinforcing characteristics of its base, the enterprise[15]. Since the terms liberalism and socialism were abused in the last century during the Cold War their meanings have to be sought in historical documents.

Liberalism as a defining characteristic of the emerging bourgeois society was the sovereignty of the market and the natural harmony of interests. As Alexander Pope put it in verse

*"Thus God and nature link'd the gen'ral frame,
And bade self-love and social be the same."*

Medieval society did not provide a soil in which the first seeds of liberalism might easily germinate. The middle ages produced a society of status in which the rights and responsibilities of the individual were determined by his place in a stratified, hierarchically ordered system. Such a closed, authoritarian order, however grandiose in outline and noble in aspiration, was bound to

---

[15] J.K Galbraith (1958) argues that a modern state even should be considered more appropriately as the industrial state because of the power and overriding importance of industrial organizations.

place great stress upon acquiescence and conformity. As new needs and interests, generated by the slow commercialization and urbanization of Europe, gained strength, the medieval system was modified to accommodate the ambitions of national rulers and the requirements of an expanding industry and commerce"(E.B. Vol. 10:846). Socialism as a defining characteristic of industrial society is a reflection of Industrialization. "Although it is possible to trace adumbrations of modern socialist ideas as far back as Plato's Republic, Thomas Moore's Utopia, and the profuse Utopian literature of the 18th-century Enlightenment, realistically, modern socialism had its roots in the reflections of various writers who opposed the social and economic relations and dislocations that the Industrial Revolution brought in its wake" (E.B.Vol.16:965).

Liberalism 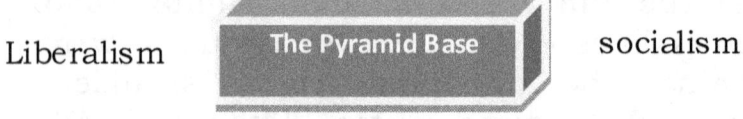 socialism

Liberalism and socialism are considered expression of interest as reflected in the enterprise and the larger society in concomitant manner[16].

Democracy, as we know it today, is the characteristic of industrial society. Its uniqueness from hitherto societies lies in its structure and function of democratic process. This can be appreciated in interest representation at the larger society level and with its integration, in its basic unit of production institute, the enterprise[17]. Postindustrial society may or may not reflect advanced form of democracy. But in industrial society, for the first time in hitherto history we find interest representation of classes and associations like professional' associations, artistic and cultural associations and farmers associations etc. working in a contextual framework of conflict and cooperation. The masses of the society *are* active in the social, economic and political life of the society. Freedom of press, thought and legal enactments of lofty principles are empty words

---

[16] Elusive forms of socialism and liberalism which characterizes the third world are different as will be shown later on

[17] Even though Spencer and Durkheim did not further what makes industrial society democratic as we put it in interest representation yet were aware of its capacity. Both thought "classes could coexist harmoniously in the industrial society, as long as these societies continued to develop their relatively open and democratic character". (E. B. Vol. 16:957)

without interest associations and their being no mechanism that the balance between different groups of interests is reflected. The reflection is in the state's enactment of laws and enforcing them and changing them. The uniqueness of the industrial society concerning democracy as we know it today is summarized below.

Athens was considered a democratic system but it was only a democracy built on enslaving the larger part of the inhabitants and it was based on a relationship of freemen and subjects.

Feudal Europe was based on the relationship of serfs upholding acquiescence and conformity and the lords order and chivalry. H Tawney (1964:22-3) expresses similar idea as follow: "The facts of class status and inequality were rationalized in the Middle Ages by a functional theory of society, as the facts of competition were rationalized in the eighteenth by the theory of economic harmonies; and the former took the same delight in contemplating the moral purpose revealed in social organization, as the latter in proving that to the curious mechanism of human society a moral purpose was superfluous or disturbing. Society, like the human body, is an organism composed of different members. Each member has its own function, prayer, or defense, or merchandise, or tilling the soil. Each must receive the means suited to its station, and must claim no more. Within classes, there must be equality; if one takes into his hand the living of two, his neighbor will go short. Between classes there must be inequality; for otherwise a class cannot perform its function, or a strange thought to us - enjoy its rights. Peasants must not encroach on those above them. Lords must not despoil peasants. and Craftsmen and merchants must receive what will maintain them in their calling, and no more.

In human history it is only industrial society which is based on management and trade union relationship the first upholding order and productivity and the later equity and egalitarianism which are manifested as liberalism and socialism, the two great traditions of democracy, as we know it today (leaving aside what post industrial society might bring). It was only industrial society that legalized the right to strike, demonstrate in general that institutionalized interest representation with the necessary instruments.

The other aspect of democracy that makes present day industrial societies unique from hitherto societies and present day industrializing societies is that its basic interest representation institute is concomitant in its larger society and at its basic unit of production, the enterprise and its interest representation is concomitant with productivity and social justice. It is not the existence of a production unit that differentiates the industrial society from the hitherto existing societies. It is characterized by:

1. Interest representation like the larger society at the enterprise level.

2. The enterprise in all miniature forms contains the characteristic of the larger society. In the hitherto existing societies in the mines and farm fields of the slave societies the relationship between the worker and the "supervisor" is not based on interest representation. In medieval society mines and agricultural fields the relationship between the worker and the "supervisor" was a relationship of serfs and lords. In the enterprise the relationship of the worker and the manager is governed in collective agreement based in interest representation by management and trade union.

3. The industrial society is the concomitant existence of its economic sustenance and advancement with its democratic system in interest representation. At the enterprise level management and trade

unions as interest representatives are the democratic institutions of the society at the same time each respectively upholding productivity and order on one hand and equity and egalitarianism on the other are the basis of its economic viability and sustainable growth.

Using this unique aspect of industrial society the DPDS forwards a development theory for underdeveloped countries.

2. THE DEMOCRATIC PERSPECTIVE IN DEVELOPMENT STUDIES AS A THEORETICAL APPROACH

"A friend of mine has said that, fortunately for college administrators, knowledge is naturally divided into units that can be taught in forty lectures of fifty minutes each." F.K Berrien (1986: 6)

The industrial society, which commenced in 19th century Europe, is a society characterized with industrial production, its unique and differentiating aspect being interest representation, (as defined in the previous chapter) concomitantly existing along productivity and social justice in its basic production unit, the enterprise. This evidenced in the larger society by the concomitant ideology of liberalism and socialism[18].

The features of the industrial society explained in the previous chapter could be summarized here under as a starting point for a theoretical approach. They are:

1. A society where productivity and order upheld by management on the one hand and equity and egalitarianism upheld by trade unions on the other hand the mechanism of interest representation in a concomitant way where the fulfillment of equity and egalitarianism requires the fulfillment of productivity and order.

2. A unique form of democracy where the relationship at the enterprise level in 1 above are expressed, in the main, in the larger society with the concomitant

---

[18] In Marx dialectical model every social system not only has an immanent force that give rise to antagonistic relations but the base and the superstructure are integrated in the mode of production which distinguishes one type of society from another.

Marx was the first man to show in a systematic manner what happens at the production site in the industrial society is deterministic to the super structure of the larger society.

existence of socialism and liberalism as ideologies of interest representation[19].

3. A fast growing and productive characteristic arising from its uniqueness in the concomitant existence of its democratic (interest representation) and economic (Productivity and order along equity and egalitarianism) imperative along the contextual relationship of cooperation and conflict with other enterprises which makes it to develop its productive forces fast compared to any society before it.

Different views were propounded about industrial society. It was related to extensiveness of industries (as an industrialization process) and others try to understand it as a chemomecanical and biological like organism as it is tried in General System Theory (GST) (F. Kenneth

---

[19] Here we are not referring that state socialism led by the Soviet Union and liberalism by the US as it is used by G. A. Borgese in his writing about world federalism but using the initial meaning of the term consistent with the idea forwarded in chapter I. "G. A Borgese viewed the cold war as a struggle about the principle of justice on which the necessary world federation would be based..by the end of the last general war (the ninth by some reckonings), only two great sovereign powers remained, Russia and America. They found themselves the bearers of the two great traditions of western democracy-liberalism and socialism." (Baratta, 1987:8)

Berrien (1968:7 -8). Others have understood it as a stage in the development of the productive forces. That may be correct for the purpose of their analysis. But here the understanding of the industrial society in the DPDS tries to unravel its aspect which could be a lesson for development studies specific to under developed countries. For people of the third world who are interested to repeat the miracle which capitalism brought about in mere 100 years in Europe, as the Manifesto has put it, such a definition is handy to forward a general theory which will serve such an end.

2.1 Industrialization and development of industrial society

It is important to understand when the industrial society came to existence and what was its development imperative. Consistent with the definition of the industrial society expounded in the previous chapter, the industrial society came to existence when trade union-management relationship commenced. In the historical approach, the later Middle Ages are taken as the starting point in the rise of trade unions from guilds. Even though development is a process, the rise of the industrial society could be assumed at the time where trade unions illegally or legally stood as organized force for wages and benefits. Adumbrations of trade unions in the later middle ages cannot be taken as characteristic of the first stage of the industrial society in its economic social and political form of organization as we know it. The later Middle Ages where management and trade unions relations have not appeared was not industrial society either. R.H Tawney correctly observed a fact, which will support our argument. ""Over a great part of Europe in the later middle ages, the economic environment was less intractable than it had been in the days of the Empire or than it is to-day. In the great commercial centers there was sometimes, it is true, a capitalism as inhuman as any which the world has seen, and from time to time ferocious class wars between artisans and merchants. But outside them trade, industry, the money market, all that we call the economic system was not a system, but a mass of individual trades and individual dealings. Pecuniary transactions were a fringe on a world of natural economy. There was little mobility or competition. There was very few large-scale organization. With some important exceptions, such as textile workers of Flanders and Italy, who in the fourteenth century, repeatedly rose in revolt, the medieval artisan, especially in backward countries like England, was a small master. The formation of temporary organizations, or "parliaments: of wage-earners, which goes on in London even before the end of the thirteenth century, and the growth of journeymen's associations in the later middle ages, are a proof that the conditions which produced modern trade unionism were not unknown. Nevertheless, even in a great city like Paris the 128 guilds that existed at the end of the thirteenth century appear to have included 5,000 masters, who employed not more than 6,000 to 7,000 journeymen. At Frankfurt-am-Main in 1387 actually not more than 750 to 800 journeymen are estimated to have been in the service of 1,554 masters."

"In cities of this kind, with their freedom, their comparative peace, and their strong corporate feeling, large enough to be prolific of associations and small enough for each man to know his neighbor, an ethic of mutual aid was not wholly possible, and it is in the light of such conditions that the most characteristic of medieval industrial institutions is to be interpreted (Tawney R.H 1960:25-6)."

Thus it is safe to assume that industrial society commenced in the 19th century. In England trade unions were established clandestinely in this period. Also for the first time in history they were legalized in 1824. Even though the legalization is not important the appearance of trade unions as interest representative of the workers in a contextual relationship with management is important for the emergence of the industrial society.

In the historical approach about capitalism and in theorizing about industrialization in modern times the well known academics are Rostow and Gerschenkron. Both of them see a prerequisite for capitalist development. Clive Trebilcock (1981) book summarizes critically the Rostow and Gerschenkron models. The Rostow Model: The Airborne economy is a stage theory or phases. "The initial phase from which the expanding economy must emerge is that of the 'traditional society', a benighted world based upon pre-Newtonian science and technology. If all goes well, this dim scenario is exchanged, in the fullness of real time, but fairly briskly in Professor Rostow's analysis, for the "preconditions stage, a form of industrial apprenticeship in which the qualifications for industrial growth are painstakingly gathered together. After this grooming process, comes, somewhat less spontaneously than the traditional industrial revolution but hardly less explosively, the stage of 'take-off'. (P. 4). The

Gerschenkron model: the deprived economy deals with backwardness. "It will be commended also by its well-developed flexibility and its modest expectations. Nothing as sophisticated as the preconditions- with their proliferating transport systems, their reforming agriculturalists, and their enterprising businessmen- is postulated as the starting point for industrialization."(P.8)

In essence, it is not the prerequisites, which we must look, but the emergence of the new organism and its nature which we must examine if we want to derive a lesson for development study. Let alone the fulfillment of prerequisites the importation of industries in massive scale couldn't build an industrial society as we observe in the Middle East. Kuwait has imported massively industries, infrastructures etc but could not be considered as an industrialized society in the full sense of the term.

2.2 The Enterprise: The basis of theorizing in DPDS.

The enterprise (or as some call it the firm, the organization) is the industrial society basic production unit as the family is the nucleus of society. The enterprise is the basic unit of industrial society because of the following reasons:

1. Productivity and order and equity and egalitarianism are the founding stones of the larger industrial society value of liberalism and socialism respectively. Like the larger society socialism and liberalism the relationship is dynamic and self-adjusting to a higher development in steeped up compromises at refined levels.

2. The relationships of the other sectors of society such as the farmers, the elite, the merchants etc. are based 'on interest forwarding at the expense of the other.

3. Interest representation in its contextual form of cooperation and conflict, which is the basic characteristic of democracy of the industrial society, finds its reinforcing and lasting base in the enterprise and the enterprise only.

4. The reinforcing nature of democratization lies in the enterprise in the relationship between management and trade union and we cannot assume modern democratic society without it. (In this age of computers and robots where the demand for labor is decreasing and if there are no trade unions to represent the working people and if management and the elite *are* to plan the society from their

lofty point of view *we* could only have oligarchy).

The enterprise in industrial society is different from enterprises in third world because of the above characteristics. This of course doesn't mean that such characteristics will be always visible in each and *every* enterprise and trade union. Here the possibility of its existence upholding equity and egalitarianism is enough. The case of trade union existence in third world countries where they don't upheld equity and egalitarianism and which are not of the nature of the industrial society is discussed in the next chapters. The present trend in Europe and elsewhere where the labor relation is outside union-management paradigm is also a bad sign for the continuity of democracy and growth.

The enterprise can be looked from the angle of productivity and growth (as an economic imperative); social well-being (as social imperative) and as the basic unit of democratic society along industrial democracy (as a political imperative) and all these are based on the nature of the relationship between management and trade unions the first upholding productivity and order and the later equity and egalitarianism cooperating and conflicting among themselves and cooperating and competing with other enterprises as one[20].

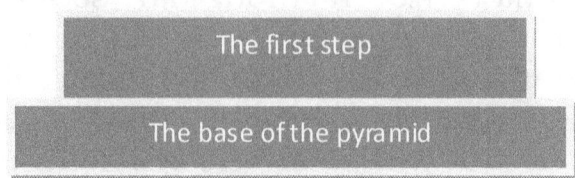

If we look at the enterprise, the history of collective bargaining will tell us how the two traditions of management and trade unions move up the step in conflict and cooperation. This does not mean that at one point the trade union upholds equity and at another time egalitarianism nor that management at one points upholds productivity and at another time order. What it means is that in the process each of them gets willing in sharing the others ideal and move to the next step.

This is because productivity cannot be fulfilled without social justice and vise versa. They happen concomitantly. Without rise in productivity, social justice cannot be attained. The case of Poland of Walesa is a good example. The workers made a "revolution" but cannot achieve equity and

---

[20] This integrated approach in developmental studies compared with the specialization approach opens a way for theorizing about developmental issues.

egalitarianism because there was no increase in productivity and it was not possible to improve their lot at the expense of the farmers since the farmers were well organized (Harrod, Jeffrey 1990:)[21]

This can be made a parody resembling a Maya pyramid. The Maya pyramidical model gets its name from the Chicanel temple-platform a four sided stepped pyramid of the Meso-American civilization. The Mayan pyramid unlike the Egyptian has stages that reach to the apex. Thus from every step on one side one can draw a line to the opposite parallel step.

Figure 1: The Maya pyramid parodying the enterprise

Looking back at historical facts management from the position of laissez-

---

[21] The point may be misleading. In the third world countries where the workers and management advance themselves at the expense of the peasants will not lead to democratization as will be shown in the next chapter.

faire attitude, a combination of laissez-faire economic thought and the protestant ethic, where management has no responsibility for the welfare of the worker outside the enterprise moved to paternalism where it is assumed that management has responsibility for the communities in which its plants are located. From here conceptions of public relations and community service and then conceptions of broad social responsibilities followed including efforts to reduce environmental pollution (E.B Vol 9:497-499).Trade unions started as associations of workers using similar skills in the late 18th and 19th centuries concerned with wages and working conditions. Then they organized themselves to national unions and the national union to federations. This growth was concomitant with the raising of larger issues such as protest against discrimination in the political franchise and the whole aspect of society founded upon class distinctions and later on worldwide democratic issues. What seems to be forgotten is that trade unions through collective bargaining agreements or otherwise are sharing management prerogatives[22]. To date collective bargaining agreements include such issues as

---

[22] The changing role of trade union and management were

a) working conditions

b) conditions of service

c) border line jobs

d) overtime work and crew complement

e) disciplinary procedure and disciplinary measures for nonconformity to production process and work place behavior

f) Profit sharing schemes and sometimes including bonuses, wages and salaries, provident funds and joint consultation procedures.

g) Job descriptions, which are part of the work contract and collective agreements, are also part of the contract of each worker and the collectivity.

In the DPDS, management and trade unions movement up the step on the Mayan pyramid sharing with each other values of productivity and justice is analyzed and scrutinized. If we take, say over time work

---

tried to be understood from a micro point of view within a decade. Take the past decade. Streeck (1987) sees it as a "normal consequence of a temporarily' changed balance of power during the period of crises." Blanpain (1985) sees it as arising from technological developments. Purcell (1983) suggests "centralized budgetary controls have profound implications for the location and control over collective bargaining".

and crew complement in the above examples, we identify the productivity and order aspect of it and put it on the left side step of the pyramid. That aspect of it, which lies in equity, and egalitarianism, which is a social justice expression, on the right side of the pyramid parallel step. Thus management and trade union in a contextual relation reach a new stage of industrial democracy.

The conspiratorial perspective considers work place democratization as stimuli from the outside either in the form of socialist revolution or the outcome of the manipulation by the trade union or management. Such view falls short to recognize work place democratization as embedded in industry itself. The contextual relation between management and trade unions representing trends, which will lead to democratization, should be appreciated. Thus we could make a typology as follows:

1. The positivist neo-Marxists who think that workers control could be used as a strategy for political and social revolution.

2. The traditionalist neo-Marxists who think that workers participation is a means of ameliorating workers into the capitalist system and it has no transformative role.

3. The behaviouralist humanist school which sees that alienation and frustration of workers could be ameliorated by workers participation schemes and that productivity could also increase by adopting this system; and

4. The school of system analysis which approaches the question at hand as a continuation of the Weberian and Taylorian method of organizing work and work process for productivity and efficiency.

On the other hand, the DPDS by analyzing them on the Maya pyramid sees each of the prerogatives give way to cooperation as we move up the stage increasing productivity at the enterprise level and growth in the larger society.

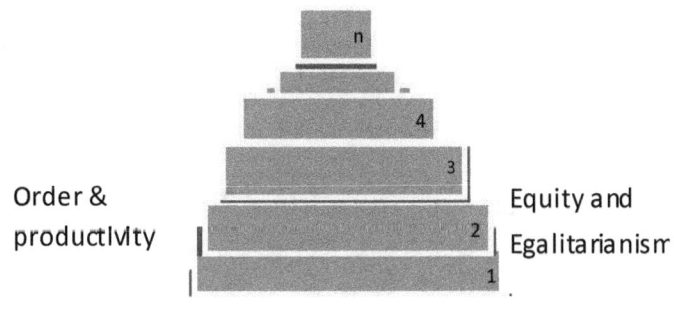

In the parody of the small Maya Pyramid above the steps are marked the steps as 1.2.3 .... n because the end result is not known. Every step shows a balance where trade unions and management have shared each other interest and then set them as their respective prerogatives onward. If we take conditions of service, borderline jobs and overtime work and crew complement in the above example they could have been taken in the prior stage or period management prerogatives. During that stage management would have not been willing to negotiate on such issues of what it considers its prerogatives. But when the steps are moved they are incorporated in the collective agreement which makes them the interest of the trade union. Trade union will assume the new position as its prerogatives which management should not act upon without its consultation. Then management will assume new positions as their prerogatives, for example work organization and method study. During every stage management will be willing to share its prerogatives with trade unions if the measure fulfils the goal of productivity and order which it upholds. Trade unions will accept the responsibility if it fulfils the interest of social justice which they stand for. Thus productivity, innovations and social welfare, which are the source of further development of the productive forces, become the interest of both management and trade unions covered up in contextual conflict and cooperation.

Is there a limit to what management and trade unions share in the due process of democratization? None. Any management prerogative like job evaluation and method study is not outside the era of trade unions. US, the UK and Sweden have witnessed, in the past, number of job evaluation schemes prepared with the active participation of trade unions (lLO 1983:9).

Thus in the DPDS workplace democratization has a reinforcing character to the further democratization of the industrial society[23]. The integrative function is seen by employers based on three basic premises as David Guest put it. He observed that

---

[23] Much of the achievement in industrial democracy was achieved in a thumb rule. The rationalization of the development was put as follow by analyzing the reason why management was willing to accept participatory schemes. In the First World War the frustration and alienation of the workers and the dumping of initiative was recognized and joint consultation to ameliorate it was introduced (Coates, Ken 1975:97).As Paul Bernstein put it structural designs of an integrative intention in human relations technique are job rotation, job enlargement. improvements in communications, experiments in joint consultation between management and workers and profit participation as well as individual share holding schemes (Bernstein 1980:5).

employers and employees have a shared interest in the success of the enterprise; that no change in the structuring and control of organization are required; and that management should be left to manage with a minimum interference from unions /government/ or other interest groups" (Guest, David 1979:306-7). Here David Guest seems to come to recognize the internally embedded democratization process in the enterprise.

2.3 The enterprise as a dynamic force of society: The basis of the DPDS in developmental studies

In analyzing the relationship between the enterprise and the larger society it is usually assumed that the larger society has the greatest impact on the development of industrial society[24]. This assumption is the basic reason for government institutional instrumentalist approach for development. State socialism built technological base of socialism that it could build communism in the future. Developing countries elites assume that they could from above bring developments that

---

[24] Even Dunlop (1972: 103-4) explaining the relationship between the political system and industrial relations takes as given the political ' system. Political systems are considered exterior power. "In a sense, "political systems" set up the major players in the industrial relations game and define their major rules of play".

are directed in preparing technological and otherwise prerequisites for capitalist and socialist development they opt. Both aimed export led industrialization or import substitution industrialization.

Outside GST, modern research about the influence of the larger society on the firm and the firm on the larger society is highly influenced by the ecological view point of Charles Darwin[25]. What he said in biology was transferred to organizations. Herbert G. Hicks and C. Ray Gullett (1975 ch.22) analyzed organizations as ecosystems by taking organization with its environment as constituting an organizational ecosystem.

The eco-system as analyzing the relationship between the larger society and the enterprise is farfetched. In the ecological relationship the part is not the characterizing feature of the whole. The enterprise on the other hand is the determining and featuring part of the whole. One of the eco systemists William M. Evan

---

[25] Biologists are also in the forefront in General System Theory. "The impetus if not the origin of general system theory came from Von Bertalnffy a theoretical biologist (1950), who was subsequently joined by Boulding, an economist (1956); J.G Miller, a psychiatrist and psychologist (1955); Ashby, a bacteriologist (1958) Rapoport, a mathematician (1956); and a growing list of persons representing a diversity of formal training and academic affiliations" (Berrien F.K; 1968: S).

(1976) in his concept of "organizational climate" writes that "The outermost circle, the social structure of society, in turn affects the culture, the interorganizational system as well as the organizational system. He also identified six prerequisites for the transformation or industrial organizations as follows: "(1)the extension of the ideology of egalitarianism from the political to the economic institutional sphere; (2) the reduction of the range of occupational skills due to technological advances; (3)the growth of informal organization that encroaches on managerial decision making prerogatives; (4)the professionalization of management; (5)the professionalization or labor; (6) the objectification of authority (1976: 20) . What we look in such analysis is that the enterprise and industrial society are taken as organism and nature and secondly that the ideology of egalitarianism is transferred from the larger society to the enterprise.

The return to Darwinism from Marx and Weber has not helped much to further the understanding of the relationship between the enterprise and the larger society.

The dynamic force in industrial society and its developmental imperative is the enterprise. The enterprise where management and trade unions stand for productivity and order and equity and egalitarianism respectively and where the fulfillment of the goal of each one of them depends on the fulfillment of the other motive and where their motives are shared in a gradual process is the dynamism of development. This fact explains the difference between enterprises of the industrial society and the "enterprises" of the developing world and the former socialist countries[26].

The dynamism of the enterprise, which arises from management trade union relationship as interest representatives as shown earlier, affect the larger society in a positive way. Such dynamic enterprises could make a difference. The difference Toyota and Sanyo etc. make in Japan. The dynamism of the enterprise also affects the components of the larger society by integrating education, values and norms, technological and infrastructural development by making their existence dependant to serving it.

---

[26] The relationship between management and trade unions in the industrial base subordinate countries is shown in chapter 3 as management upholding order and loyalty and trade unions livelihood and justice with their own concepts of the defining words.

2.4 The larger society: The manifestation of socialist and liberalist traditions

Liberalism and socialism as concomitant phenomena of the industrial society were introduced in chapter 1. The analysis of the enterprise on the two interests of management and trade unions was forwarded to lead to the analysis of the industrial society in detail towards bringing development to the developing countries.

Collective bargaining was used to emphasize the role of trade union and management. Management dedication for productivity and order the trade union motives for equity and egalitarianism in collective agreement proved their concomitant existence in the enterprise. The existence of socialism and liberalism as characterizing features of the industrial society could be demonstrated as follows:

The first is a historical based one as was stated in chapter 1 where the ideology of the emerging bourgeoisie was liberalism, the sovereignty of the market and the natural harmony of interests, and socialism as an opposition to the economic relations and dislocations the industrial society brought about.

The second is the struggle between market economies and planned economies which takes its form at the national level in opposing state interference and at the international level between the soviet model and the capitalist model. In his writings about world federalism G.A Borgese even viewed the cold war "as a struggle about the principle of justice on which the necessary world federation would be based .. .... by the end of the last general war (the ninth by some reckonings), only two great sovereign powers remained, Russia and America. They found themselves the bearers of the two great traditions of western democracy- liberalism and socialism" (Baratta. 1987: 8).

The third is the day today activities of political parties and interest groups as they raise the issue of productivity and welfare. In the larger society, *we* find many interest groups such as occupational, cultural, recreational associations, regional associations along trade unions and management unions and farmers' interest groups. All influence the policy of the state. What makes the socialist and liberal traditions to come out is the relative balance of the relative strength of these interests vis-à-vis each other. In the industrial society, these relations and relative strength get their expression in law enactments and the behavior of the state. Either social justice gets the upper hand or liberalism wins the day but in a historical context, both *are* advanced. Lets look the following enactments: Repeal of legal prohibition of workers association was done in Europe between 1824 to 1884. Departments or ministries of labor *were* established in Europe from 1806-18 and in US in 1913. Labor law consolidation (not codification) in Europe was done from 1910 to 1919. Labor relations act was passed in US from 1935- 47.

The enactments show us the growing trend of social justice but at the same time productivity was rising. *The* state in industrialized society is the reflection of the relative strength of the interest groups in a democratic process embedded in the enterprise.

We could start to parody liberalism and socialism in the larger society in a straight line as follow:

Liberalism   The Maya pyramid base   Socialism

The line is open ended because *one* cannot parody developments on a straight line but in stages of parallel lines. It is best exemplified by a steeped up pyramid: the Maya pyramid we introduced for analyzing the enterprise.

The Maya pyramidical model

In *the* typology, as was done for the enterprise, *we* draw thus *the* features of liberalism and socialism as they move up the stages of development.

Socialism   Liberalism

Every step on the Mayan Pyramid is not a new social system. It is a stage of further development of compromises for social justice and the rise in productivity. The single linear progression and the process of dialectical change failed to express it. Here the spirit of development is not at war with itself like Hegel said or the society at war with itself like Marx said but in a continuous and contextual relationship of conflict and cooperation to attain the general goal.

The reinforcing nature of the system arises because to fulfill socialist goals a simultaneous development from the liberal end has to be realized. Social justice to improve and take the next step a simultaneous increase on the other end, which enables liberalism to move to the next step, productivity improvement, is required. In such a process the steps are moved in a continuous developmental process on the continuous step of the Maya pyramid. This development will have its ups and downs. If productivity is not growing then social justice will be hampered. At this juncture upward movement is not only impossible but a backlash may happen. Marx understood these ups and downs as a dying throbs of a system born to die. Even though there are ups and downs the growth in a contextual process which continues along the Maya pyramid.

Heuristically speaking we can divide the stages up to now into 6 in the European and U.S stage. They are not laws but some sketches for discussions.

- 1824-1900 where the balance was in favor of liberalism, Labor laws are enacted to protect the interest of the propertied class. In almost all countries working class associations are prohibited. In the theoretical field, Marx's Manifesto and Capital are published.

- 1900-1917 Where socialism has gained ground over liberalism; this is characterized in the theoretical field with Weber's declaration that the working class is not ready to assume power and suggests liberal imperialism as a class collaboration technique in Germany. Departments and ministries of labor affairs were established.

- 1917-1947 The Russian Revolution haunts Europe, In U.S labor relations act were passed. Workers participation schemes in the west starts. Socialist democracy and wage policy as state capitalism measure of socialism is strengthened.

- 1947-1960 The cold war era starts; with the weakness of state socialism unveiled liberalism assures itself that the seed of the future lies not in the proletariat but in management.

- 1960-1982 Socialism on the retreat, theories on social movementism and union free management appear.

- 1982- to the present - Liberalism assumes that the defeat of state socialism is the victory of liberalism - the sovereignty of the market and the natural harmony of interests.

The stages show that both systems are promoted even if it appears one or the other is gaining advantage over the other.

The lessons drawn in the relationship of the enterprise and the larger society in the industrial society and the integrated aspect of its economic social and political imperatives are important for development studies. Present day industrial societies may be more complex than the Maya pyramid, which was made as a parody, but it helps to understand the industrial society in order to get a lesson for industrialization.

2.5 Cross cultural studies in the DPDS

Cross cultural studies, like the analysis of the relationship between the larger society and the enterprise, is influenced by the eco-system which is a unidimensional approach. The following quotation summarizes it best. "One may look at two dimensions that are provided by the environment of the organization and two dimensions that are provided by the internal life of the organization. The "outside" dimensions arc (1) the social structure of the country and (2) the sentiments and value orientations characteristic of the culture. The "inside" dimension are :(3) the structuring of interpersonal relations and (4) the distribution of rewards and penalties "(EB Vol. 9:499).

Cross cultural studies in the DPDS, on the other hand is the function of analyzing different societies in their respective position to industrialism. Societies could be classified as industrial base subordinate or industrial base dominating. In between we find shades of the classifications. The DPDS analyzes this condition in a linear model.

This could be observed by taking the "enterprise" in different societies at different stage of development and comparing it to the enterprise of the industrial society. The relation between management and labor in the underdeveloped societies is not that of productivity and order on one side and equity and egalitarianism on the other with its deterministic impact on cross cultural studies of industrialization. In the "enterprise in the underdeveloped countries management upholds order and loyalty and trade unions livelihood and justice. As we go on the line we find countries that are in between.

The linear model of cross cultural studies differs from Kerr et al. model in that it does not take technology and industry as causal primacy[27]. A country like the oil rich Arab

---

[27] Comparing the similarity of the technologies used in US, Japan, and Britain Dore (1973), Hamani (1980) and White and Trevor (1983) analyzed the difference in the mode of work organization, industrial relations and rule making as arising in the different cultural traditions of the societies. Brian Twiss (1988), G. Blinsky & M.A Hills (1985) showed that quality circles group technology originated or evolved outside Japan. But this doesn't mean that if technology is not the causal primacy then the values of the larger society are the causal primacy. R. Blanpain (1990) shows a case where Ford U.K failed to introduce team work,

countries may import industries but they are not industrial societies.

The linear model of cross cultural studies

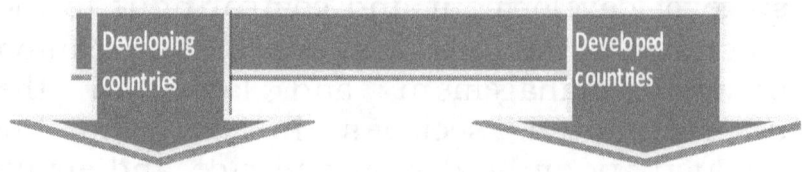

Industrial base subordinate   Industrial base dominant

According to the DPDS perspective the culture of the enterprise more dominant in societies where the industrial base is dominating and in societies where the industrial base is subordinate the influence of the larger society is more dominant in modifying the theories and practices of management and management labor responses to them[28].

---

harmonized pay structure, more employee involvement and more flexibility while it was successful to implement these same things in another plant. F Lardner says about Japanese "They applied logic and common sense to their problems rather than laboratory investigations and discounted cash flow calculation" (Blinsky G & Hills, Moore A, 1985: 290).

[28] Attitudes based on the culture of a society are also important. I. Ahiauzu (1984) in his study of Nigerian

In industrialized societies the culture of the firm is dominant because the enterprise is the basic setter of the norms and values of the larger society. The relationship of the enterprise and the larger society is that of the family to the society. On the other hand in societies where the industrial base is subordinate the enterprise is an island in traditional mode of society. Since it is subordinate it is more influenced by the traditional values of the larger society than it influences the workings of the larger society.

In the DPDS cross cultural study of the so called industrialized societies the same unilinear model is used. If we take Russia, Japan, the Anglo Saxon England and the US and Western Europe the DPDS analyses them in their relative position to industrialism. The difference between Japanese management practices and the relative position of trade unions as interest representatives vis-à-vis the other interest representatives is analyzed taking into consideration the remnants of traditional values and norms during the push to industrialization to catch up with the West. The

---

Workplace identifies culturally based attitudes in regard to authority, desire to acquire material wealth, individual need achievement motivation, attitudes to formal education, orientation to wage employment, attitude to class distinction, attitude to face to face interpersonal relations and general attitude to change.

same is with Russia. The DPDS in such a way explains why management and labor relation practices show difference in industrialized countries.

2.6 *Positive and Negative Impacts*

The DPDS by forwarding the inherent nature of democracy to the enterprise and arguing against voluntarism doesn't mean to do away with positive influences the state and management and trade unions could play in industrialization, industrial democracy and industrial relation.

Positive influence arise from understanding the inherent working of a system. Negative influences from voluntaristic endeavor. The following are some of the voluntaristic measures we witnessed in the last 70 years. In Yugoslavia, Marshall Tito introduced workers participation scheme to ameliorate Stalin's ideological stance and it ended in failure of productivity and order.

Workers control and workers owned firms were established in many countries and they ended up in not fulfilling the productivity, equity and egalitarianism aspirations of workers and society.

State socialism was established to enhance the transition to communism and its failure was so shocking it set back the developments of democratic traditions of industrial society i.e. order and productivity on the one hand and equity and egalitarianism on the other.

Theories forwarded in debate with Marx being refined into a threatening force of trade union existence thus with a great impact on interest representation structure of·-the basic democratic tradition of industrial society.

The developing world elite by trying to simulate the Soviet block and the West for fast industrialization has left on its heels shattered societies.

In the industrialized society positive influence lies not in breaking the basic pillars of its democratization process. Such a danger is arising from social movementism and certain sector of HRD on the one side and revolutionarism on the other. The first threatens the existence of trade unions the second by relating democracy to the question of ownership tries to create an oligarchy of elites to guide society by nationalization.

As the social political and economic imperative lies in the enterprise relationship between management and trade unions and at the larger society expressed in the relative outcome in the stages of liberalist and socialist balances; so positive impact, whether conscious or unconscious comes from the recognition of the interdependence of the enterprise and society. Classical perspective of management, repeal of legal prohibition of workers associations and the years 1824 – 1900 where the balance was favorable to liberalism go together. Human Resource perspective in management (1930), establishment of departments or ministries and labor relation acts and the aftermath of the Russian revolution where socialist ideas were on the upsurge demonstrate the fact.

The above can be made into typology by taking the positive and negative influences to industrial democracy, management, trade unions and the state relationships.

| Productivity & Order | The Maya Pyramid Base | Equity & Liberalism |

In this model, the struggle between the two traditions is taken as leading to industrial democracy. The two traditions are enforcing each other. We could develop the model by adding the democratization of work with the democratization of internal trade union practice. Both are reinforcing each other.

Democratization of workplace reinforces democratization of trade union practices.

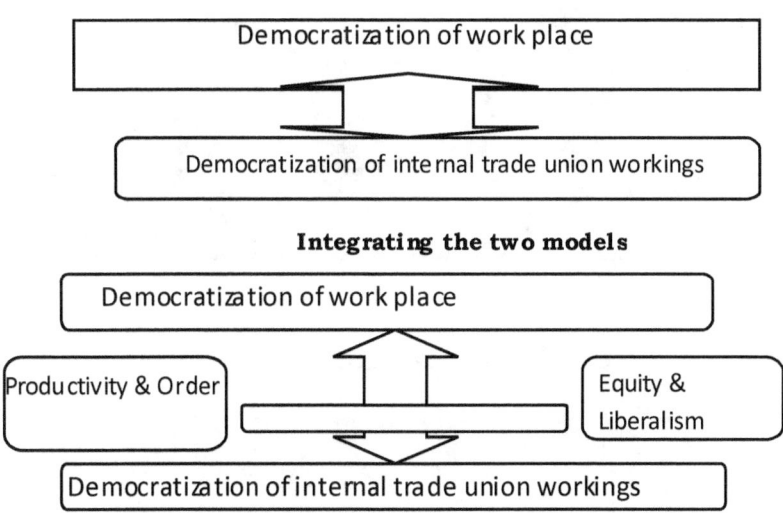

Integrating the two models

The positive and negative impacts in each of them enforces negative or positive influence respectively. When management, trade unions and the state show positive impact work place democratization, growth in productivity and internal trade union democratization and enterprise whole offices democratization is enhanced.

Therefore, we could have the following positive and negative impacts models:

Negative Impact

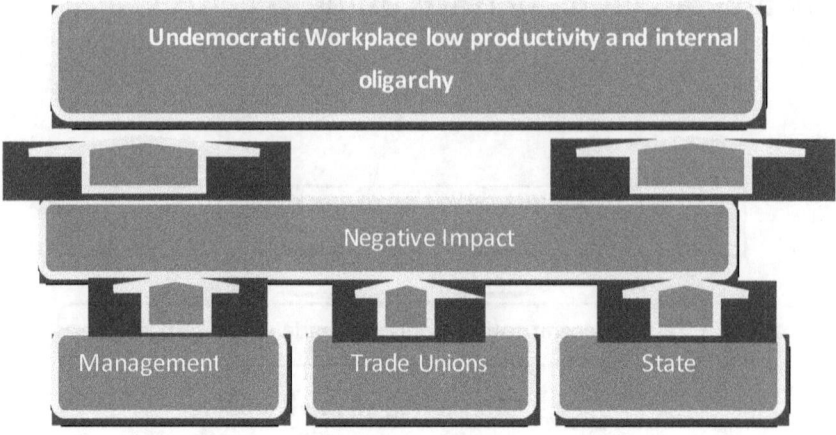

Positive Impact

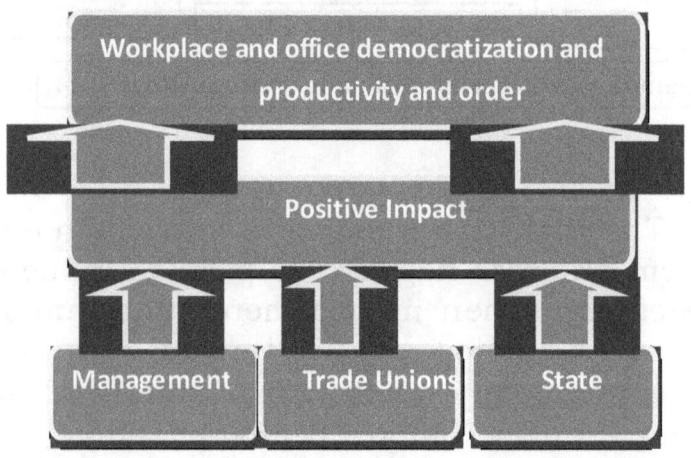

3. RELEVANCE OF THE DEMOCRATIC PERSPECTIVE IN DEVELOPMENT STUDIES

"We must carefully distinguish between the effects of the colony trade and those of the monopoly of that trade. The former are always and necessarily beneficial; the latter always and necessarily hurtful."

Adam Smith

There are four wrong assumptions about the third world industrialization that arose from wrong similes and analogies.

The first wrong assumption is that the "enterprise" in the third world is taken to be similar to the enterprise in the industrialized countries. The similarity in technology is taken to give rise to similarity in the relationship between management and trade unions and the whole aspect of the industrial relation system. Kerr et al. have influenced this kind of idea, the counter arguments about the viability of this assumption were based on empirical observation, and it has not developed to a general theory.

The second wrong assumption is that once industries are established in the third world countries industrialism will get its momentum and industrialization is on a firm footing. This assumption arose from the grand generalization that civilization starts from a centre and disseminate. The industrialization of Europe in the 15th to 19th centuries and the advancement of industrialization and industrial society from few centers is the general similarity in cultural developments. Thus for comparative studies for the development of the non-industrialized societies the following happenings have to be emphasized: 1) Urbanization in quality and coverage, 2) Elaborated state bureaucracy, 3) Participation of the mass of people in social and political life, 4) The culturalization of industry. These factors enabled new technologies and working methods to be assimilated and disseminated in continental Europe and even to be taken by the migrants to the New World.

The third wrong assumption is that the third world larger society could be transformed to a democratic society we know in the industrialized counties by simply adopting multiparty systems and the free market principle. This assumption arose from the widely held view that democratic principles disseminate into the enterprise when analyzing the relationship of the enterprise and the larger society in the industrialized countries (chapter 2).

The fourth wrong assumption is that there is a certain material prerequisite that is needed to give an impetus to industrialization. These prerequisites are dominantly of material base and it downplays the nature of the unit of production, the enterprise, in industrialization[29].

The best approach in studying the "enterprise" in the third world context is to look at it as an independent entity and

---

[29] It is a concept transplanted from evolutionary theory to social science with no relevance at all. It does not need empirical data to know that any amount of prerequisite fulfillment will not give rise to an organism, which is thought to be the result of the fulfillment of the prerequisite. Say monkey to man. But this does not mean that traditional society cannot transform to industrialized society. That is a possibility which history witnessed in the transformation of Europe and why this paper is written.

compare it with the enterprise in the industrialized societies. Some have tried to understand the enterprise in the third world by using concepts which have different meanings for different cultures. A research team from Philips N.V, which conducted a study of this type, found out that the terms could mean different things in different settings.

"In a project in Tanzania, for example, we mean by ecology the physical location, local materials, and infrastructure, by culture the employees' membership of tribes and its impact on attitudes and behavior, by technology radios assembling with the required skills, and by power the financial resources and results, budget control, and relationships with government and customers. In two projects in France, we mean by ecology the distance from Paris and the resources of subcontractors and labor in the region, by culture the value orientation of French managers based upon tradition, education, and class membership, by technology development and production of clock radios and electrogramaphones for special markets, and by power the same as in Tanzania" (Hesseling, Pjotr 1969:230).

3.1 The enterprise in the third world

In chapter one and two the relationship between management and trade unions in the industrialized society is featured by the first upholding productivity and order and the later equity and egalitarianism. But the case in the "enterprise" in the underdeveloped world is different.

From the outset adumbrations of management as standing for productivity and order in the underdeveloped countries exist as it is manifested in the "free zones" which produce for export purposes and in countries which are said to have export oriented industrialization strategies. Barring exception, "enterprises· in the third world countries amass profit not from productivity but by exploiting price mechanisms in a monopolist structured economy.

In Import Substituting Industrialization (ISI) the "enterprise", the infant industry, is protected from competition. In ISI, domestic enterprises are encouraged by "extreme currency overvaluation combined with quantitative restrictions provided the equivalent of prohibitive tariff protection; techniques of allocating import licenses were employed which prevented competition among domestic firms and reward entrepreneurs for license-getting abilities rather than their cost-minimizing performance; and excessive and detailed quantitative controls were employed over many aspects of economic activity" (Krueger, 1990:99). Krueger analyzes the anomaly which competition for import licenses in such an industrialization strategy creates and observes that "Empirical evidence suggests that the value of rents associated with import licenses can be relatively large, and it has been shown that the welfare cost of quantitative restrictions equals that of their tariff equivalents plus the value of the rents" , (Kreguer, *1990:146).*

On the other hand, in Export led industrialization, the enterprise is not protected from internal competition but subsidizing it is also a practice. But in the whole the enterprise is encouraged to compete. The main support it gets is the right to exploit the workers at a lower wages.

So in the developing world we have two dilemmas. In ISI we have protected industries where the main issue is not competition and productivity and in ELI we have a condition where the "enterprise" is forced to compete in a world where the absence of international free trade and non-discriminatory monetary system is a disadvantage which led to the cooptation of the trade unions and/or outlawing trade unions.

3.2 The protected "enterprise" in ISI and the downtrodden worker in ELI: Dilemmas of the third world in productivity and equity

Thus in ISI in the developing world we have enterprises where the normal relation of management and trade unions in industrial societies couldn't be practiced. In ISI we have a protectionist policy for the infant industries where management's prior motive is not productivity and order but order and loyalty and trade unions stand for livelihood and justice. If not identical with this paper's view but a similar type of relation was observed by Greet Hofstede (1984:87). "In more collectivist culture, the relationship between the employee and the employer has a moral component. It is felt to be similar to the relationship of child with its extended family where there are mutual traditional obligations: On the side of the employer, protection of the employee, almost regardless of the latter performance; on the side of the employee, loyalty toward the employer .. " Jon Kraus (1988: 172) observes about the co-opted trade union leadership by the state in third world where the union leadership is conservative and distance themselves from the rank and file membership. Ronaldo Munck (1988: 112-13) wrote, "trade union leadership sees its achieved status as a means to upward social mobility". In ELI we have productivity and order upheld by management and trade unions forced not to stand for equity and egalitarianism or are abolished finally. Thus in ELI we have management standing for productivity and order and in the absence of trade unions or their subservience position the workers are forced to succumb to order and surveillance as the only practical day to day livelihood.

InImport Substitution Industrialization

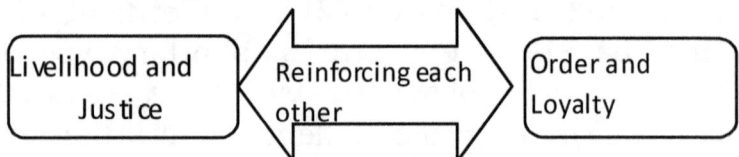

In Export Led Industrialization

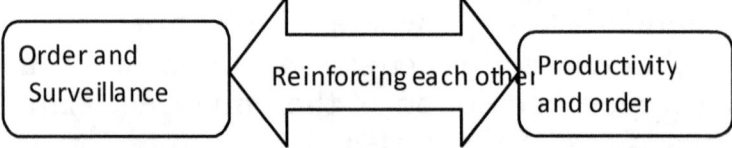

The inverted Pyramidical model in ISI

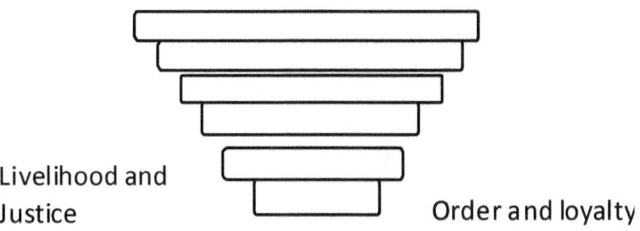

Livelihood and Justice

Order and loyalty

Here livelihood and justice have their own meanings. Livelihood means to have money enough to buy the niceties of life which are better of than the rural population. Justice means a due share of the profit the enterprise makes. Since profit does not grow up from productivity it means sharing the extra profit accrued from price increases for most of the time. In this condition the priority for management will be order and loyalty rather than order and productivity. Even though empirical researches on this line are not well developed some researchers have studied the impact of ISI and it can be used for this paper argument. "Using detailed Colombian earnings data. T. Paul Schultz (...) analyzed the impact of protection on earnings of workers and employers in Colombia. He concluded that a large portion of effective protection went to providing quasi-rents to both employers and workers in protected industries. With a 10 per cent increase in effective protection raising workers' wages in those industries by about 3 per *cent,* compared to comparable workers in non-protected industries and employers wages by an even larger proportion (.. .). Schultz regarded these effects as largely income-distributional, implying that much of the effect of protection is to build in quasi-rents which then accounted for a significant portion of observed wage differentials for workers of comparable education and experience. To the extent that the quasi-rent effect of trade regimes is important, that would suggest that the income distribution becomes more unequal under an inward-looking strategy, but that effect would not influence the demand for labor per se"(Krueger, 1990: I 27).

Thus the so called enterprise in the third world of ISI is different from the enterprise in the industrialized societies in the present context as well as during their industrialization period centuries earlier as follow:

1. It lacks the economic momentum which leads to the growth of the productive forces and sustainable drive.
2. It doesn't help the growth of socialist and liberalist culture in the larger society which is necessary to build industrial

society or to start momentum of industrialization.

The industrial relation concept is a reflection of this reality in the underdeveloped countries. This is not to mean that there are not "industrial relation practices· but it is to emphasize they are different from the industrial society. Caricatures of tripartite, the bipartite systems along flamboyant arbitration laws, courts and ministries to oversee them could be found in Third World countries.

Industrial relation in such a society has also its own peculiar feature which could be observed by the day to day activities of the industrial relations officer:

1. The work of the industrial relation officer is to promote paternalistic relation with the workers and with their trade unions.

2. Promote good liaison with local authorities, police and courts to enhance the paternalistic relation with the workers and their trade union and cooperate with the government in perpetuating the system.

3. Promote the importance of the enterprise in the developmental process. Since there is almost no competition, salesmanship and participation in community development are not important.

4. If the work is not full time for the industrial relations officer responsibilities of a personnel officer and a legal advisor or that sort of thing are added up.

HRM as understood in most third world countries following ISI strategies could be fairly assumed to have been relegated to such position. Such a system could be transformed only by a conscious measure which will change the relationships at the enterprise followed by the transformation of the relationship of interest representation in the larger society.

Since the relation between management and trade unions is not based on productivity and order on the one hand and equity and egalitarianism on the other, the Maya pyramidical model couldn't be used. It is rather parody by the inverted pyramidical model of the Maya Pyramid where values of livelihood and justice on one hand and order and loyalty on the other without productivity rise and social justice expand filling the spectrum without bringing industrialism.

The stepped up rectangle in ELI

The countries following ELI are not in a better condition. Management because of competitiveness in a world environment where tariff barriers and non-convertibility of currencies demands it to sacrifice the social justice aspect of the management and trade union relationship which is observed in industrialized societies.

The relationship between management and trade unions in this instance can be parody in entrance steps of the gothic church.

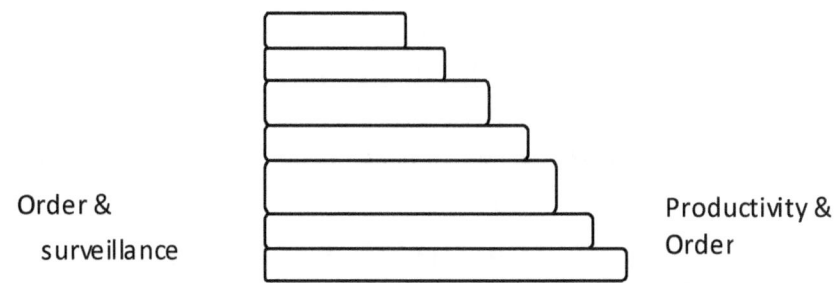

Order & surveillance

Productivity & Order

While every step in productivity and order is moved up the step on the other side order and surveillance is perpetuated. This condition of anomaly in the developing world better explains why structural adjustment programmes (SAP) of the IMF and the World Bank cause too much hard ship in the developing world.

Thus the so called enterprise in the third world ELI is different from the enterprise in industrial societies in the present context or during their industrialization period centuries earlier for the following reasons:

1. It doesn't help the growth of socialist and liberalist cultures in the larger society that is necessary for building industrial society or to start the way to industrialization.

2. The relationship between management and trade unions as it is different from the industrialized societies at present and during their industrialization period doesn't lead to sustainable development of the productive forces materially and culturally.

3.3 The larger society in the third world

The larger society in the third world has also to be analyzed for what it 'is worth and then compared to the industrial society at present and during its industrialization period centuries earlier. The history of the late and early times have much to tell us about the inherent capacity of societies. History has also a lesson how industrialization became a culture of a society. In Europe it took roots in three locations. Italy is known for the artistic renaissance of the 15th century. Germany for the rapid growth in mining, metallurgy, trade and the invention of printing by Gutenberg, the Spanish and Portuguese looking for gold and for the legendary Prester John in Ethiopia were led to the discovery of the New World. The age opened up the development of science and ushered in bringing science to the realm of politics, the Enlightenment, and by the end of the 18th century the rapid economic change in England was caught up by the continental powers. The enlightenment centered in France, was fought in the realm of power politics. "During the 19th century industrializing Europe assimilated the consequences of the rapid industrial development in England and the lessons of the enlightenment. Modern urban society developed in one nation after another with a constantly improving industrial base, elaborated state bureaucracies for regulation of trade and welfare, and increasing participation of the mass of people in social and political life[30].

---

[30] The name "industrial revolution" was first coined by French writers in the sprit of an obvious metaphoric rapprochement between the political cataclysms of the French Revolution and the period of rapid economic change in England. Although the term was extra-Marxian and even pre-Marxian in origin, it fitted well into a system of economic thought which showed so much interest in the discontinuities of historical process"(Gerschenkron A, 1979:93).

After the Second World War much of Europe was destroyed and rebuilt again. The argument that without Marshall Plan the west couldn't have been reconstructed is half truth. It was effective since it was applied in a society which have developed human resource. "Marshall Aid was spectacularly successful in removing trade barriers, promoting recovery of output, establishing international reserves and collective action to provide credit" (Maddison, A 1989). Somalia is now destroyed by civil war and its rebuilding capacity is unthinkable at least from the inside. Thus, the all out development in human resource is a more important base for industrialization than money and instruments. Now Somalia may have more university graduates than 18th century England. Still rebuilding will be hard without bringing the human resource from outside and the rebuilding will not amount to building industrial society. Industrial society is not developed because a country has a lot of industry and infrastructure but by the inherent and the uniqueness of industrial society in its integrated structure from the enterprise to the larger society.

Kuwait and the Gulf States have industries but they are not industrial societies as we know it in its entire feature. The sustenance of their economies depends much on cartel trade and with the integration of the world economy and the order of free trade and the enforcement of market mechanisms their economy could be endangered if they don't start building industrial society by transforming the "enterprises" and the larger society in their countries. Industries, even if numerous, may still remain an island in traditional society. This recognition is necessary for development studies in the Third World. The following is a typology of third world conditions.

What makes industry an island is not that it concentrates in few centers. This is much true of the developed industrial societies too. The main reason is that the enterprise as well as the larger society have not an inbuilt mechanism that characterizes the industrial society. A good analogy about society's capacity is traditional farming. If there is war and whole instruments of farming are destroyed the traditional society after the war can build them as the Europeans built their industries from scratch after the Second World War.

What makes the developing world different from the developed is not that there are fewer industrial establishments but basically the industrial base is subordinate to the traditional mode of production and the "enterprise is not geared to productivity and social justice in the sense of the industrial society and thus lack the internal dynamic for the growth of the productive forces and the equity motive of social justice. So, heuristically speaking we could compare them as follows:

Industrial base Subordinate		Industrial base dominating

In the line we find the LDCs at the first stage and at the end of the line the industrialized societies. The middle position is occupied by those on transition. For the present analysis the oil rich kingdoms along the LDCs lie in the first stage of industrial base subordinate.

In countries where the industrial base is subordinate the larger society's value pillars are not socialism and liberalism and in the enterprise it is not productivity and order on the one hand and equity and egalitarianism on the other. The larger society is much characterized by traditional values which bind expression in acquiescence and conformity and order and chivalry.

Acquiescence   Order &
& conformity   chivalry

[diagram: horizontal bar between the two labels]

Acquiescence and conformity at the larger society means different things for the people of the third world countries following ISI and ELI even tough they are not basically different. In ISI it means acquiescence and conformity to the system (whether it is ISI of a capitalist orientation or the necessarily ISI of the socialist oriented countries) so that the condition of the workers for livelihood and justice could be fulfilled and the peasantry squeezed. Here the ideological stance could be state socialism or nationalism for a faster growth. In ELI acquiescence and conformity means sacrificing livelihood and justice by the working class for competitiveness in the world market. Here the ideology could be nationalism of the Pancasilla type that is reflected also in the industrial relation appealing to the peasantry or an outright illegalization of trade union activities.

This typology may not seem from the outset elegant. But non industrial society cannot be otherwise. This is where Kerr et al. made their mistake when they forwarded their idea of the causal primacy of technology and industry and the guiding hand of the elite. Whoever (elite or otherwise) guides the society the end result is the same.

The system based on one hand on acquiescence and conformity and on the other hand order and chivalry must be the point of concentration in developmental studies. The larger society in the third world couldn't be assumed to uphold the two traditions of socialism and liberalism in a contextual relationship of conflict and cooperation. In ISI the socialist oriented countries calling themselves socialists and the capitalist oriented ones calling themselves liberals and standing against the bourgeoisie and the communists respectively is the inheritance of the cold war politicking which has no practical significance in the values of the larger society. The system does not start up sustained industrialization. The pillars of the industrial society on the one hand productivity and order on the other equity and egalitarianism one or both of them are sacrificed at the enterprise level and socialism and liberalism at the larger society level. Adumbration of socialist and liberalist ideologies in the third world are the result of the power block politicking or of utopian nature. Both cases of ELI and ISI, in the current situation are characterized by one or many of the following anomalies:

1. National economic boundaries[31] and high tariff systems keeps it from competition and productivity. The role of trade policy and trade strategy in promoting growth is not web researched but "empirical evidence overwhelmingly indicates that there are important links between them" (Krueger, Anne D, 1990:95)."Nonetheless, experience has clearly demonstrated the importance of access to international markets in providing a means of permitting more rapid growth than would otherwise be

---

[31] The artificial boundaries that are the result of colonialism or historical accidents are wrongly taken as the boundaries of a nation state in the order of Europe during industrialization and industrialism. This is justified by the revolutionary elite by quoting Lenin and Stalin's nationality question and the arising of the nation when capitalism develops even though there is no industrial society built. The former and rational bases of a country where different non-centralized administrative units cooperate in facilitating trade and counter military invasion are thought as worthless. A non- industrialized society where religion, region comes first and country second is transformed artificially as if the country comes first then religion and region second like industrialized society. This serves for building tariff walls and discourage competitiveness in production.

feasible. Given the enormous difficulties and costs of achieving the institutional and other changes that economic growth requires, it is probable that trade policy changes have a higher rate of return to LDC's than most other feasible policy changes. It is, of course, to be hoped that protectionist pressures in the developed countries do not result in fewer opportunities for the LDC's. If such protectionist measures are taken, they will lower the rate of return to outward-oriented trade strategies. They will however, for the foreseeable future, still leave that rate distinctly above the returns from a policy of persisting with inward-oriented growth (Krueger, 1990:101).

2. Through the mechanism of nationalization of rural land and the limitation of credit institutions the masses of the people are put outside capital. The capital of the peasants in the third world is land. Even where revolutionary land reforms are instituted the buying and selling of land is forbidden and the peasants cannot use it as collateral to get credit from the bank (socialist oriented countries). In other countries where

land reform has not been implemented the peasants have no capital to be used as collateral. The result in both cases is the same.

3. By making the national currency not subject to changes in world markets an island of a nation is created where wage anomalies, along with its effect on development are perpetuated. "There are also important links between the nominal exchange rate and the real wage. It can be argued that, in some countries, a depreciation of the nominal exchange rate is effective precisely because it lowers the real wage, at least in terms of traded goods. Turning that proposition around, an overvalued exchange rate in a labor-abundant country may make the real wage sufficiently high to reduce or wipe out comparative advantage in labor intensive industries, and devaluation may in effect be an instrument for lowering the real wage. Even further complexities are introduced if wages are indexed in terms of domestic currency in highly open economies."

"From all of this, it is plausible hypothesis that rapid growth in demand for unskilled labor will occur when the labor market is permitted to function freely in the context of a reasonably open trade regime and a realistic exchange rate (Kreuger, 1990:120)[32].

4. By competing with the industrialized countries which could be of similar status when a poor man competes for show up with his rich neighbor the extraction of surplus from the population creates a condition where the living status of the people is kept low and with a negative effect on cultural development.

5. The rule of utopian elites who pass as working class or masse based (the peasantry and the traditional ruling class characterized as such) governments. The elites think of their people as having no capacity to know their own good and have to be guided by their "learned" daughters and sons.

---

[32] This anomaly in the economy along the supply and demand problem it creates is the basic reason for the lowered wage of workers in the third world. On one hand the protected industry discourages the production of substituting or similar goods which creates the problem of supply and the shortage of goods in turn will lead to inflationary prices and to keep down inflation wages have to be put down. The condition is similar to that of a dog running in circles to catch its tail.

3.4 The Third World: Simple problems exaggerated polemics

The dilemmas of the third world are simple and they beg common sense solution. They are not riddles of the ages. But the problems are approached from wrong perspectives. Solutions forwarded either doesn't strike the problem or they address half of the problem. Servicing the debt is approached in institutional adjustment without considering the institutional requirements necessary to stop the capital flight[33]. Transforming the production relations are taken without considering the need for development of the industrial society.

The industrial system in much of the third world can be typology in the above inverted pyramidical model.Here the two pillars don't get narrower but they expand up to filling the whole spectrum of the society without industrial society being built. Any measure which threatens it to change their relation to be based on productivity is opposed by both sides. Such pressure usually comes from international organizations like the IMF for structural

---

[33] In the Sudan the debt of the country is almost equal to the capital flight from the country (Brown, Richard 1991).

adjustment purposes or from certain version of nationalist or "Marxist" regimes. The first usually tries without changing the whole aspect to make the enterprise competitive with the world market, and when it tries to make it competitive inside the country it fails since the analysis starts from wrong premises of the sovereignty of the market prior to the break up of tariff barriers and artificial national boundaries. The latter ones by forcing the people in industry to live as low as the peasants and forego consumption or by trying to motivate the workers at the expense of the peasants tries to build many industries and infrastructures. Since this will not be accepted willingly the reign of terror accompanies it.

In both condition the state which has opted for it will be collapsing with armed uprisings or it is characterized by coup de eat of recurrent nature which makes it as similar as the preceding state which is characterized with this hazards since the workers and/or peasants upheaval always needs to be ameliorated with the change of office bearers through coup de tat or cabinet reshuffles.

In the DPDS thus it is taken that there is no industrial society in the developing world and the industrialization process needs a positive influence. Negative influences from whichever direction and motive have to be discouraged. The best positive influence is productivity bargaining in industrial relation in an environment of free 'trade and without tariff walls and an integrated currency and free flow of goods and services.

3.5 The transformation: The way to industrialization

The transformation of the "enterprise" in the developing world by making management to upheld productivity and order and trade unions equity and egalitarianism in the two industrialization strategies needs the same type of general structural adjustment[34]. In ISI where productivity has to be emphasized and competition to be encouraged the social impacts will be overcome by free trade and in ELI where equity and egality have to be emphasized the productivity of the enterprise for the sake of increase in wages and benefits could be encouraged by free trade and the dismantling of the protectionist brier and the improvement in the international monetary system.

---

[34] This measure will be the end of the ISI and ELI industrialization strategies which arose in the world of protectionism and unequal exchanges.

3.5.1 The transformed enterprise

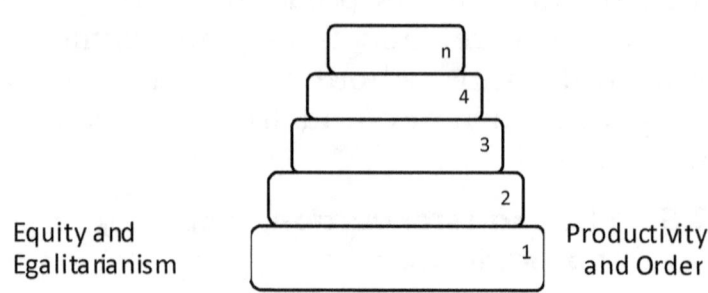

Industry once out being a parasite on the peasantry and /or workers, the management to survive will uphold productivity and order and trade unions will upheld equity and egalitarianism. This could be corporate from the present experience of the former socialist countries like Poland and East Germany. Socialist values and orientation become the main values of the rank and file workers as it learns that scapegoat creation will not solve its problem. Nor it will be possible to forward ones own interest at the expense of the peasants.

The relationship between the state and the enterprise with trade unions and management in industrialized societies and the developing world is different. In the industrialized societies the state is the expression of the relative strength of management and trade unions basically and its role in influencing the management-labor relation is limited by the inherent characteristic of the society. On the other hand the state in a developing society could play a major role in positively influencing the overall development of the society one of it and not the most important being management labor relation.

Productivity bargaining in such an environment would change the basic relation between management and labor from livelihood and justice on the trade union side and order and loyalty on management side to equity and egalitarianism on trade union side and productivity and order on the side of management. Concomitantly this will change the larger society.

3.5.2 The transformed larger society

The transformation in the enterprise will force the pillars of the larger society to change to a different thing if not similar to industrialized society. What is socialism on one hand and liberalism on the other in industrial society will be substituted by equity on the one end and liberalism on the other. This is likely because during the first phases industrial base will be subordinate and the society demand will reflect the agrarian demand tempered with industry. The peasants once free from state control for extraction purpose and their destiny in their own hands rather than their "learned" sons and daughters could organize themselves based on interest representation. Let's parody it:

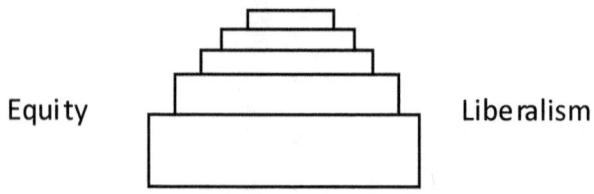

Such happenings could be predicted from the late experience of the former socialist countries. In Poland where productivity was not the main issue when socialism collapsed. During the change, the demand of the workers for increase in real wages was frustrated because increment was possible only at the expense of the farmers and the farmers union was able to protect its interest. Thus the state was forced to balance the interest of the farmers and the workers and management. Since industry was not the dominating characteristic it did not emerge with management and trade union values as pillar of the society.

The next chapters will take the transformation process in detail, keeping in mind that it is a logical deduction and that in practical life there will be many other things to be considered.

4. THE DEMOCRATIC PERSPECTIVE IN DEVELOPMENT STUDIES AS A POLICY IMPERATIVE

"were it not for the unwarranted generalization that all control is wrong, we should deal with the social environment as simply as we deal with non-social. We accept the fact we depend upon the world around us, and we simply change the nature of the dependency. In the same way, to make the social environment as free as possible of aversive stimuli we do not need to destroy the environment or escape from it, we need to redesign it."

B.F. Skinner

The question of transforming the third world has remained a contested issue. Many ideas were suggested about improving the situation of the third world. Genville Clark and Louis B. Sohn proposed a World Development Authority years back. The World Development Authority under the U.N. Economic and Social Council is suggested to be established "with powers to make grants in aid or interest free loans to governments or organizations for economic and social projects considered necessary for the "creation of conditions of stability and well-being". The Chicago committee suggested a World Planning Agency (Beratta, J.P. 1987:8-9). The IMF pushed for structural adjustments. J Fitzgerald and Vos (1988:2 I) argue for international policy coordination, recycling of the Japanese and German trade surpluses to developing countries, debt relief and write off assessing that this would lead to a higher demand for third world exports and reduction of international interest rate and generate, new lending but cautioning about LDC's borrowing from private lenders. Paul Streeten 1987: 1481) took the problem as a social and natural problem and wrote that " in a regime which income, wealth and power are unequally distributed, the poor suffer whatever policies are pursued." He looked back at the lessons of Marshall Aid and suggested independent experts trusted by both donors and recipients and genuine transnational secretariat as a possible solution. The optimistic wish about world industrialization by the year 2000 had already failed. Hopelessness and pessimism about the third world, especially about Africa, was no more whispered but talked aloud. Mark Duffield in 1991 in a conference about the Horn Of Africa had written that if progressive reform is lost "the alternative is that during the 1990s, whether national governments like it or not, Africa's position in the new world order could crystallize as a welfare annex of the West" (Duffied, Mark 1991:22). Both donors and recipients of aid, both institutional structuralists at international level and at the other end the countries directly concerned seem to lack a way out. This is because lack of a general theory which could guide policy and procedural developments.

4.1 General Structural Adjustment as alternative

A good case in point is structural adjustment programme (SAP) forwarded by the IMF and the World Bank. SAP has raised the concern of many people who see its cause and rationale in different aspect. Campell and Loxley argued that it is a policy drawn from " a distorted interpretation of how the newly industrialized countries had successfully adopted export oriented strategies"(campell & Loxley 1989:2). Jeffery Harrod argued that "the leading investing nations and businessmen, working through the IMF, sought to execute the policies for repayment of the impudent and insecure loans made a decade earlier" (Harrod, Jeffrey

1990:21). According to Singer (1989:3) Breton Woods Agreements contained the germ of the current debt crises. The IMF and World Bank's institutional approach was directed to devaluation of the inflated currencies of the third world, (but not their currencies convertibility), and making competition and the market the guiding principles. The reform was limited to the developing countries and did not proposed corresponding reform at the international level). The problem was that it only addressed half of the problem. SAP doesn't address the problem of flight of capital from the third world to the first world, nor the convertibility of the currencies of the third world and the institutional instruments for their structuring. Thus it doesn't address the need for structuring of the first world in order to balance the anomalies in the third world. When third world countries negotiate with their counterparts, says the EEC, they raise the case of trade and tariff without relating it to structural adjustment and without relating the advantage of structural adjustment if it goes with international free trade, convertible currencies, i.e. international monetary reform. Adjustment with a human face is felt but the know how about the way out seems to be absent.

The persistence of such lack of coherence around the world about development and the pessimism about the underdeveloped world suggested that a general theory, and a new one, is needed.

The reevaluation of the role of capitalism in the third world got its momentum after Gorbacheve's assent to power. Priority to agriculture and the traditional path of initial industrialization and even suggestion that there are no viable alternative to capitalism in the third world countries, surfaced in the Soviet Union during this time (Muchie, Mamo & Zon, Han Van 1989:193)[35]. The disintegration of the bipolar political order opened possibility to look for alternatives development strategies.

---

[35] For trade unions in the North the question of social justice' will be characterized in decreasing working hours, the encompassing of part time workers in its union and cooperating with social movements for its struggle at continental or country status and in its international relations with trade unions in the South the advancement of world governance based on equity and legality. For trade unions in the South the important issue is to cooperate with their governments for getting trade and tariff concessions, convertible international monetary structure and the strengthening of the UN as a democratic institution where the interest of the South could be represented fairly. The abolishing of trade and tariff barriers throughout the world and particularly between countries in the South is also important.

The DPDS based on the theoretical approaches described in earlier chapters draws alternative policy imperatives. The DPDS proposes General Structural Adjustment Program (GSAP) contrary to SAP which is directed lopsidedly to the developing world. Thus DPDS recommends that the transformation of the relation of management and trade unions in the third world from that of order and chivalry and livelihood and justice to productivity and order and equity and egalitarianism requires structural adjustment programmes of the types the IMF is running now plus additional structural adjustment programmes to be implemented by both the developed and the developing world. The additional structural adjustments require international cooperation too. Thus a general structural adjustment programme (GSAP) is a universal approach. GSAP has three purposes.

1. The changing of the inverted model by changing the relationship between management and trade unions from *order* and chivalry and livelihood and justice to productivity and order and equity and egalitarianism, to create a momentum of industrialism, in the developing world.

2. The changing of the values of the larger society through general structural

adjustment measures from acquiescence and conformity and *order* and chivalry to socialism and liberalism to create an industrializing society[36].

3. GSAP at international level would create a new world order based on cooperation and the wellbeing of all humanity.

4.2 **General structural adjustment Program (GSAP) defined as a concept.**

General structural adjustment (GSA) is a tool for the democratic perspective in development studies. DPDS concept which has an implication of transforming the "enterprise" and the larger society in the third world will transform the relationship between the Third World and the first world. Thus GSA can be defined as institutional instrument and monetary and political measure aimed at transforming the underdeveloped countries economic, social and political system for the purpose of making industrialization a function of industrialism.

---

[36] The underdeveloped world cannot be taken as travelling on the path of industrialization as Kerr et al. suggest in the DPDS as long as these relationships persists.

General structural adjustment is a function of related but integrated components with economic, social and political imperatives.

The enterprise and the larger society are integrated in industrial society since the enterprise is the basis of the larger society (chapters 1&2). In the same way if the "enterprise" in the underdeveloped countries is to be a growing influence on the larger society adjustments are of a two-pronged drives[37].

Thus GSA requires not only to changing the "enterprise" in the underdeveloped countries but also the promotion of national, regional and international free flow of goods and services (absence of tariffs), making the third world currencies susceptible to world market ups

---

[37] AS long as the enterprise in the under developed world remains of a relationship of justice and livelihood on one hand and order and chivalry on the other and not equity and egality on one hand and productivity and order on the other hand the value of the larger society in the under developed world will remain flawed. It will be characterized by closed national economic boundaries, high tariff, nationalization of rural and urban land, and limitation of credit. The non convertible currencies in the developing world will be vulnerable to ups and downs in the world market, and absence of civil society.

and downs (convertibility) and to achieve these goals upheld a political stand of world federalism based on justice and equality among and between countries.

4.3 Free Trade international monetary intern and World order

A Madisson (1989) identified four phases of development: The liberal world order to 1913, Conflict and Autarky (1913-50); the "Golden Age"(1950-73) and phase IV as Growth Deceleration, and Accelerated Inflation. What makes his four phases interesting for this paper is that the points raised could be used along their empirical data to prove that the underdeveloped world does well during periods of free trade and in an international monetary system, which is stable.

The first and the third stage are characterized as liberal world order. The later one known as a new liberal world order. In both phases there was a successful dismantling of trade barriers, fast growth of international trade, unhindered private capital flow and possibilities of international migration.

Phase two and fourth are worst years. They were characterized by shocks. The first with the world wars and the later with the oil crises. In the first international monetary system collapsed, liberal trade policies were replaced by discriminatory blocks, absolute fall in foreign investment. In the later phase the Breton Woods fixed exchange rate collapsed, new sets of objectives were set[38].

The underdeveloped world has a lesson to learn from the experience of its ex-members. The oil rich countries seemed to be well off with increasing income at present which seemed unsustainable. *The* East Asians who integrated their economies to the world market are better off than the others.

GSA in the DPDS is thus a function of transforming a society to a relation of productivity and order and equity and egalitarianism at the work place and at the larger society and world level to liberalism on the *one* hand and socialism on the other. The words socialism and liberalism here are used in their initial meaning as was indicated from the start. *Some* researchers have tried in the past to take the soviet system as socialism and tried to see the emergence of the market led and planned economies as concomitant existence that will lead to a new world order - world federalism (Braatta 1979). Others have seen the merging of the two economic systems as a

---

[38] The most interesting outcome of this period is SAP.

new model for the East and West (Ellerman: 1990). In the 1980' social movementism was replacing world federal movements - the strengthening of the UN system into a world government. Today this issue is gaining ground as we see in the talks about new world order and the role of the UN. From the point of view of the third world strengthening the UN system, advocating for a new world order based on basic democratic principles and cooperating with social movements in the North to enhance a democratic world order is a political imperative of a very great significance.

Today like the second and the fourth phases in Maddison's typology it seems *we* are witnessing the end of the fourth phase with the collapse of the state socialist system, the disintegration of the USSR and the throes of a birth bang of a New World Order nobody has tried to define it in a concrete way. *The u*nderdeveloped world could playa role in its definition by adopting the DPDS as a policy imperative in international relation. This will be World Federalism with free trade and abolishment of tariff barriers, reform in international monetary system and interest representation in the UN if not on equal footing with the advanced countries and yet to have an influential presence. The underdeveloped world in this instance has to uphold equity and egality (socialism); which is free trade, no tariff barriers and international monetary system as a policy imperative and the industrialized countries will uphold liberalism which will be characterized as preferential trade status, discriminatory blocs and will oppose international monetary system. This seems surprisingly the opposite of what we were discussing as liberalism and socialism as a concept during the initial stage of capitalism. The reason is that *the* developing countries are starting industrialism and from a disadvantageous position and secondly they are like the workers in the capitalist countries whose interest is well kept by free trade since they will get things at lower price in free trade and productivity is hampered by this measure. Adam Smith's argument for free trade at *the* initial stage of capitalist growth is a point at hand.

4.4 GSA- As an integrated approach

GSA is an integrated approach since reform in *one* aspect cannot bring change. It approaches both sides of the problem. The institutional and functional instruments should cut all related problems, say, not only debt servicing but also capital flight. Not only establishing industry but also making it instrument of industrialization[39]. The weakness of structural adjustment programme of the IMF and World Bank arises from this aspect. So is true about policies programmes of world federalists' suggestion about the establishment of "World Planning Agency" and "world Development Authority".

The third world could not be transformed from the outside unless the workplace and the larger society develop internal momentum of industrialism. The GSA programme is an integrated package of structural changes where one will not work without the other. A good example for this point is the case of *free* trade.

Free trade is *one* aspect of GSA but it has been argued too by many classical economists, Adam Smith being the giant, but it was also the policy of the US at least up to 1968 (Blinder 1987:110). Blinder raises a question about free trade and answers it himself as follow: "Did something about the world economy change to weaken the case of free trade? I doubt it. But something else did

---

[39] The West's industrialization was able to make a significance stride within 100 years while the third world has lost a century without much stride and what ever achieved not being sustainable and culturalized by the societies.

change. The special pleading of the vested interests who benefit from trade protection now get a far more sympathetic political ear than they did a decade ago. Protectionism has acquired a political respectability." (ibid: 11). He also puts the viability of free trade in a simple and beautiful way: ' .. But to understand why, we must look beyond the abstract argument for or against free trade to the specific lists of winners and losers from protection. Then we will see that trade protection secures concentrated and highly visible gains for a small minority by imposing diffuse and almost invisible costs on a vast and unknowing majority. That makes protectionism at once economically gruelers and politically fetching" (Blinder. ibid:112)[40]. Thus in GSA the use of free trade is possible only when the currencies of the underdeveloped world is convertible. So too free trade and convertible currencies could contribute positively for the growth of "enterprises" (foreign or national owned). It

---

[40] "Adam Smith explanation about free trade is simple. The truth as it is simple it is easy to grasp. "It is the maxim of every prudent master of a family never to attempt to make at home what it will cost him more to make than to buy .. If a foreign country can supply us with a commodity cheaper than we ourselves can make it, better buy it of them with some part of the produce of our own industry, employed in a way in which we have some advantage" (Blinder. ibid: 112).

will lead them to be competitive. It would discourage their dependence as parasite on peasants and workers. This requires the availability of credit and as a guarantee privately owned land property (since this is the main capital in the underdeveloped people) and homes to be denationalized or distributed fairly (reform). In the ideological field GSA requires confidence building which is lacking in the underdeveloped countries. Negative influences of former colonial rulers and internal tribal, religions chauvinism has to be discouraged from being a fetter on development.

Democracy is another aspect of GSA. The third world in the last 50 years was dominated by the post colonial elite and this situation has not helped in the development of civil society. The third world may have a lesson to learn from the EEC structures and workings. The Economic and Social Committee in the EC comprises representatives of employers, workers, farmers, carriers, traders, craftsmen, members of cooperatives. Small businessmen, members of the professions, Consumers, conservationists and members of community associations (Moreau. Jacques. 1992:9). The expansion of the role of similar organizations in the third world will have a positive and advantageous impact rather than ethnic based associations and liberation movements which characterized the cold war era in the third world.

4.5 Impact DPDS on a policy based on social classes and groups

The impact of DPDS based policies on social classes and groups could be appreciated hypothetically. Free trade, convertibility of currencies etc. will have positive impact on the social classes through inducing adjustment of prices and encouraging productivity of enterprises.

It has been the underdeveloped world that was promoting tariff systems and protection of enterprises in its territories (even though much of them are foreign and are treated as scapegoats for underdevelopment) from competitiveness. The foreign and local enterprises are not locally and globally competitive in the third world.

From a point of logic general structural adjustment will not only require national owned enterprises to be competitive in the internal and external market but also the foreign owned enterprises to be locally and internationally competitive. The competitiveness of the ISI and ELI enterprises world wide and locally along with free trade practices will enable farmers and workers to buy commodities cheaply. This condition will lead to an overall development by creating viable enterprises on the one hand and increasing the purchasing power of the farmers and workers. The peasantry will be better off because it could get cheaply materials from the world market for its production and labor and it has not to shoulder artificial and baseless so called industrialization drives.

Internally the mandarin classes and the petit bourgeoisie will be a looser in the shorter period. The importance of the use of hammer and nail, saws and planning machine, the work of the cart and the wheel and the use of fertilizers and irrigations etc. during the transformation period will lead to the advancement of technical staff.

Employment will be better served in GSA because foreign investors will find nearness to market and cheap labor to be advantageous in a world where free trade and convertible currencies will make the market forces important.

The abolition of capital flight from the third world will at least encourage convertibility of currencies. According to one study the debt of Sudan and the amount of capital flight are almost equal. The enterprising class in the third world will thus be encouraged to invest internally.

GSA as a political imperative will guarantee the stability of the third world governments since they will be democratically elected and subject to a world body through the process of world federalism

The world is not yet a united block after the collapse of state socialism. But to work towards its unity of purpose and goal as human endeavor is to be encouraged

SUMMARY

The problem of third world industrialization is taken by some theorists as arising from its imitativeness of the enterprises in the West. Others have assumed that once industries, enterprises, are established in the third world industrialization will take its momentum. Still others have assumed that the fulfillment of certain preconditions in the environment of the enterprise will enhance the industrialization momentum. Nothing is far from the truth. The Enterprise, the unit of production in the industrial society, in the third world is very different from that in the industrialized societies and here lies the reason why industrialization has become a failure.

In this paper industrialism, industrialization and industrial democracy are taken to be the function of management and trade union relations when the relationship is only based on management upholding productivity and order and trade unions equity and egalitarianism which is reflected in the larger society by the two great traditions of industrial society: liberalism and socialism.

Industrial society is unique from the societies preceding it and the third world societies which have industries but which cannot be called industrializing societies. The paper by basing the productivity and sustainable growth of industrial society in a unique type of management and trade union relationship at the enterprise level and liberalism and socialism at the larger society level, forwarded a development theory. This was done by reexamining the history of capitalism from its inception in order to derive a lesson about development. It was shown that the development of the industrial society follows a Maya pyramidical model rather than a linear or a curvature one. The Maya pyramidical model gets its name from platform temple of the meso-American civilization which has stepped up sides rather than the straight-line triangular Egyptian pyramid. It was shown that every step is moved up when management and trade unions share their respective prerogatives, which have different content at different time of development of productivity and order and equity and egalitarianism respectively in the process of their contextual relationship of conflict and cooperation.

This relationship as an economic, social and political imperative is made to parody on the Maya pyramid. As an economic imperative it was shown that the technological innovations. productive forces development as the function of this relationship. N a political imperative the relationship was shown on the pyramid as industrial democracy progresses when management and trade unions share in what were in one time considered their prerogatives and move to a higher step where new prerogatives are set at which in time their sharing leads to development. As a social imperative the impact of the relationship in the enterprise and the enterprise to its environment was shown to have a positive impact on the liberal and socialist tradition of the larger society.

So to the medieval and ancient societies were compared with the industrial society and the working of the industrial society was abstracted and set. This was used to analyze the industrialization of the third world, from the perspective of development studies about the third world, as an entity by itself breaking the dilemma of making development study an appendage of cold war power politicking and being tested in theories which are primarily developed to understand industrialization in the west. In chapter 3 it was shown that the so called third world is not on the track of industrialization by showing how it has strayed far from the path of industrialization by not adopting the industrialization and fast development of the productive forces which is inherent in the enterprise and the larger society of an industrializing society witnessed in the history of industrialization of the West.

The case of countries following ISI and ELI was examined where it was shown that the relationship between management and trade unions in ISI is order and loyalty on one hand and livelihood and justice on the other respectively. In ELI management upholds productivity and order and trade unions and in their absence, workers, order and surveillance. The protected "enterprise" in ISI and the downtrodden worker in ELI were analyzed as the dilemmas of the third world in productivity and equity keeping in mind the balanced nature of these two values in an industrializing and industrialized society to create the development of the productive forces. The negative effect of the nature of management and trade unions in ISI was shown in the inverted Maya paramedical model where the system perpetuates itself without creating an industrializing process or the development of the productive forces. In case of ELI the situation was made to be parody the moving step of the Gothic church where order and surveillance are perpetuated even when productivity and order is achieved. In both cases an industrialization process is not to be achieved. In both cases the larger society upheld contextually acquiescence and conformity and order and chivalry which are the expression of the larger society of a preindustrial society. These have hindered the starting of industrialization. The need for transforming these relationships at the enterprise and the larger society is then discussed. In chapter 4 the problem of the third world which is made to look like riddles of all times, like when considering the problem of debt and the problem of capital flight as if they are not related or the utopian urge to catch up and the reality of lagging further back are considered and general structural Adjustment (GSA) is forwarded to solve the dilemma in the theoretical field. GSA is directed to change the enterprise and the larger society in the third world to gear it to a momentum of industrialization.

The policy imperative the DPDS reached by logical deductions based on the nature of the industrial society enterprise and the larger society from the initial point strengthens the arguments of the proponents of free trade, standard international monetary system, structural adjustments, and world governance[41]. But the DPDS goes further by making them: a single Package- a package for a new world order[42].

The new world order should be liberal in the sense that it abolishes tariff barriers, reinstate strong international monetary system, and the free movement of capital, goods, services and people. It should also be democratic in the sense that the UN is strengthened and the South could have a say on its destiny, the South become politically stable and civil society instated. It should be developmental in that it should demystify knowledge and policy from cold war power block politicking. This may be a hard task to achieve. But the DPDS may be

---

[41] DPDS Das for example says the following about the need for a free trade regime " the level of economic efficiency achieved in an economy is determined by the degree of openness. and the trade policy package adopted by the developing country in question and the trade policies also have a decisive and measurable impact on employment and output" (Das. Dilip K. 1990: xi)

[42] In the mid-1970's, Argentina, for instance, embarked on a reform in liberalizing domestic financial market, external trade, and capital flow and to some extent liberalization of domestic labor market (LI, Carmen & Pradhan 1990:98) but it failed to achieve its goal in the long run. The reforms were done in the absence of standard international monetary reform, free trade etc. But GSA is a single package.

a contribution to a new thinking - a new thinking about the issue of development study about the South and the well being of all - North or South.

Postscript

I will like to mention three viewpoints which I came across in the last twenty years. The first concerned the fragmentation of farm plots that are sufficient to support a single family. This is a problem the world knows for centuries and which haunts the developing world. It is rampant in countries with high birthrates. While we were discussing this problem with a Dutch gentleman he shared me the experience of the Netherlands many centuries ago. He said that once the land property reached undividable stage through applying standard for its capacity to support a family, the division had been stopped . If a family had three children the land will be passed to one of the children and the other two have to go as soldiers or priests to the colonies or participate in the colonial campaign. Europe and USA with a low birthrate and booming economy have not faced such a problem in the twentieth century. China has addressed the problem through the one-child policy. The developing world has to address the problem in a radical way.

The second is news consisting of different viewpoints that the mass media has taken up as its editorial. The financial crisis in developing countries is pushing some unemployed people to look for work in the less developed countries or their former colonies.

The third impressive development happened in Ethiopia. In the highlands the defragmentation of the miniscule land through inheritance to many descendants has made sustenance of farming in small holdings unfeasible. The country has overall unoccupied land but cannot pass it to people from the highlands because it was classified under different ethnic regions. Thus Ethiopia to address its food problem is giving big tract of lands to foreigners and tries to create non agricultural employment for its unemployed and underemployed population. No one could answer rationally why the ethnic regional governments are willing to give land to foreigners while rejecting similar demands from fellow Ethiopians other than their ethnic groups. The distribution of land to foreigners is but condemned by human right watchers as land grab.

I raised the three points in order to show that solutions are not easy for problems the world faces at this point in time. All the three cases were nation-state driven. The nation state seemed miniscule to address problems that the world faces today.

A. The Rationale for Globalization

1. The problems the world faces today are similar to the problems Europe faced in the 18th century and during the Industrial Revolution. Unemployment, social upheaval characterized Europe before the colonial campaigns for search of livelihood. The instrument for such expansion was the nation-state. The powers may clash against each other but their search for livelihood, market and raw materials were common to all of them. A nation state in today's world could not sustain its population livelihood at the expense of other nations and people like it was done during colonialism and empire expansion. The effort should be addressed in a win-win approach amongst nations and people where problems are addressed wisely and where everybody benefits[43].

---

[43] World government and globalization are the strategic goals of developing countries. If we take global problems "of nuclear war, traffic in armament, erosion of human rights, the international debt crises ,worsening poverty in the underdeveloped world, international terrorism, over population, environmental pollution, and the militarization of space ... the solution for the problems needs global approaches and mechanisms specific to its need.

2. The rational for globalization is the possibility of joint developments among and between nations. The building of infrastructures, the opening up of economic sectors in less developed countries could be done through joint effort of the developed and the developing nations. The people of both nations will be beneficiaries. Employment will be created for all of them. The movement of population from one corner of the world to the other will be characterized for joint economic development and not for colonial domination and exploitation[44].

3. The developed countries could not address their financial crisis and unemployment by employing their population in renewal of their infrastructure without triggering hyper inflation because of national currencies

---

[44] From the World federalists the Chicago Committee, more radically, provided for an extensive bill of rights and duties, a broad grant of powers, a world planning agency, and a clause permitting public purchase of business that had acquired the "extension and character of a transnational monopoly" (Bratta ibid; 8-9). Minister of Development Mr. J Pronk during his address in Salon de ideas on November 1, 1991 forwarded a 14 points agenda which suggested the establishment of an economic security council under the UN like the Security Council.

that are limited in scope. To address the problem there is a need for global understanding on the convertibility of all currencies to a single standard.

4. The sustenance of the national framework has made the application of measures to hasten youth employment by decreasing working hours and decreasing the years for getting pension scheme had proved impossible in the developing world. In the contrary measures are being taken to increase the age requirements for pension schemes. Thus also requires unemployment anywhere has to be addressed globally than nationally.

B. The possibility of Global Economic and Social Well-being

1. Developments in the last two centuries have created conditions where people could freely move and countries cooperate for development. The United Nations systems, the different regional associations could be hastened to realize the economic and social well-being of the population of the whole world.

2. Technologically it is possible to open new areas for development through infrastructure building, inducing technological and scientific application in modern farming and industry which if done concomitantly could lead to universal industrialization and urbanization and world governance.

3. Politically it was possible for USA to mobilize the whole world for a new governance where the UN grew into a world parliament with full power based on international constitution where every country would be subject to the constitution and judged in international court after the end of the Cold War. That opportunity was lost when the Unipolar world returned to multipolar world. The failure was starkly shown when consideration of the big eight and the big twenty powers was forwarded and a security council with twenty members was considered as a democratic practice. It was not different from the cartoon by Sir David Low, mentioned in the preface, about the chair for five big persons while the three was occupied. An opportunity will come again as it had happened after the Second World War and the end of the Cold War. We should not

loose that opportunity by getting better prepared.

C. The way forward

1. A new world order is the only way out for solving the crisis the world is facing at present. The economic problem is very threatening. It is disturbing more than the fear of atomic annihilation during the Cold War.

2. The new world order has to unleash the slumbering developmental possibility that could be comparable to what the industrial society did during its rise centuries before. As was quoted from Marx in the first chapter "The bourgeoisie, during its rule of scarce one hundred years, has created more massive and more colossal productive forces than have all preceding generations together. The new world governance can open employment opportunities for all and open through reconstruction and infrastructure development and scientific advancement taking humanity to a new level of prosperity and bliss.

Writing this postscript I recognized that the thesis written twenty years ago has relevance today. I think every thesis must found such opportunity to come to light.

The way forward should not be a repetition of what happened in the aftermath of the Second World War. David Low's cartoon of the time has depicted what happened to the League of Nations and the newly created United Nations when the idea of world governance based on federalism and egalitarian principles gave way to a national and group competition.

Wars, upheavals, revolutions do not lead to democracy and world governance as it was proved in history and as we are witnessing in the Arab springs and the different battlegrounds in the name of democracy. The way for democratization is through the democratization of workplace and the larger society.

The best guarantee for democratic development is the economic development, social advancement in legality, freedom, dignity and most of all sustained peace and social accountability of citizens' and government' to the welfare of all and each citizen. The individual citizen should be encouraged to stand for his right and for the right of others before legal courts and in public places.

REFERENCES

Ahiazu, A. 1.
1984 Methods of job Regulation In Nigerian Workplace A Study of Cultural Influences On Industrial Relations. Vol . 22 No 1

Baratta , J.P
1987 Strengthening The United Nations A Bibliography on U.N Reform and World Federalism . New York, Westport, Connecticut, London : Greenwood Press .

Barbash , J
1990 The Future Of Industrial Relations as An Academic Field in <u>The Future Of Industrial Relations In Eurppe</u>, W,J Dercksen (ed.)

Bernstein I Paul
1976 Workplace Democritisation; Its Internal Dynamics . Kent State University Press .

Berrien , F.K
1968 General and Social Systems . New Brunswick, New Jersey: Rutgers **University Press.**

Blanpain , R
1990 Labour Relations in a Changing Social and Technological environment,

in The Future Of Industrial Relations In Europe Proceedings Of A
conference in hODour of Professor W Albeda W. J Derckson editor.

Blanpain, R
1985 Structural Adjustment And Industrial Relations: Labour Law Aspects in
ILLS labpur and Spciety Vol 10 *H2*

Blinsky G & Hills Moore A.
1985 The Information Technology Revolution Oxford: Basil Blackwell.

Blinder A.S
1988 Hard Heads, Soft Hearts 2nd edition Massachusetes: Addison- Wesley Publishing Company.

Blumberg, Paul
1968 Industrial Democracy The Sociology Of Participation. Great .B.ritain:
Garden City Press Ltd .

Brown, Richard
1991 Debt Adjustment and Donor interventions In Post War Horn Of Africa:
Issues on The Research Agenda. ISS Working shop paper presented in Feb
19-23 1991

Burris, Val
1987 The Neo-Marxist Synthesis of Marx and Weber On Class . In ~

Issues in Spciplpeical Thepry. London , New Delhi : Sage Publications

Caircross, Alexander
1976 The Market and The State. In the Wilson, T & Skinner, A <u>The Market and
The State Essays in Honoyr of Adam Smith</u>
Great Britain: Oxford

Campbell, R & Loxley, J
1989 Structural Adjustment In Africa. London : The Macmillan Press Ltd.

Churchman, C. W
1971 The Design Of Inquiring Systems: Basic Concepts Of Systems and
Organization. New York, London: Basic Books, Inc .• Publishers.

Coats Ken
1975 Democracy and Workers' Control. <u>In Self Management: Economic Liberation of Man</u>. Editor J. Vanek. First published as Democracy and Workers'
control. In Towards Socialism. Edited by the New Left Review, Collins, 1966.

Daft, R.L
1988 Management, Cryicago: Dryden Press.

Das, Dilip K.
1990 International Trade Policy: A developing Country Perspective. Hong Rong: Macmillan.

Duffied, Mark
1991 The Internationalization Of Public Welfare: Conflict and The
Of the Donor/Ngo Safety Net. ISS workshop paper presented Feb 19-23, 1991

Dunlop, J. T
1985 General Theory Of Industrial Relations in <u>Industrial Relations Systems</u>, London: Southern Illinois Press.

Dunlop, John T
1950 Wage Determination Under Trade Unions. Oxford: Basil Blackwell.

Dunlop, John T.
1972 Political Systems And Industrial Relations. In International Institute For Labor Studies Bulletin No. 9, Geneva: International Institute For Labour Studies.

E.B vol
1975 The New Encyclopedia Britannica in 30 volumes. 15th edition.
USA: Encyclopedia Britannica Inc.

Ellerman, DPDS
1990 The Democratic Worker-Owned Firm: A New Model For the East and West. London: Unwin Hyman Inc.

Evan, William M.

1976 Organization Theory Structures, Systems and Environments. New York: John Wiley & sons .

Fitzgerald, Jansen & Vos, R
1988 Structural Asymmetrics, Adjustment and The Debt Problem . <u>In ISS Workipg Papers Series On Money Finance and Development # 28</u>

Galbraith, John K
1967 The New Industrial State. London: Hamish Hamilton

Gerth, H & Martindale,D
1952 In their Preface to their translation of Max Weber Ancient Judaism.
Illinois: The Free Press

Gerschenkron, Alexander
1952 Economic Backwardness In Historical Perspective. <u>In The Progress of Underdeveloped Areas</u> edited by B.F Hoselitz. Chicago: The University of Chicago Press.

Gerschenkron, A
1962 The Impact Of The French Revolution Upon The Lower Rhine Textile Districts. In <u>Economic History Review</u> 1

Geschenkron, Alexander
1979 Economic Backwardness in Historical Perspective. London:the Belknap Press of Harvard University Press

Gorz Andre
1973 Workers' Control Is More Than Just That.
In <u>Participatory Democracy
in Canada</u> edited by G. Hunnius 1973 Black
Rose Books republished in Hindefeld and
Rothschild Work Place Democracy and Social
Change 1982
Boston: PS publishers.

Gorz, Andre
1982 (b) Farewell To The Working Class and
Essay On Post Industrial Socialism. London and
Sydney: Pluto Press

Guest, Davidand Knight, Kenneth
1979 Putting Participation into Practice.
England: Gower Press.

Harrod, J
1987 Industrialization, Productivity and Multiple
Power Relations: Lech,
Lula and Kwan (available from author).

Harrod, Jeffrey
1990 The World Social Economy in The 1990s (
available from the author).

Hesseling, Pjotr
1969 Analyzing Industrial Organizations In
Cross Cultural Settings: A case

Study Of a Multinational Corporation in <u>Modern Organizational Theory</u> A. Negandhi (ed.) The Kent State University Press .

Hofstede, Greet
1984 Cultural Dimensions In Management and Planing. In Asia paci~ Journal
of Management January 1984.

Hoselitz, Bert F
1952 The Progress of Underdeveloped Areas. Chicago: The University of
Chicago Press.

International Labour Organization (ILO)
1983 Meetings of Experts On Pay System. Geneva 21-25 Nov. 1983.
Background Paper prepared by the ILO RESR/1983/D.1.

Kelly, John
1988 Trade Unions and Socialist Politics . London, New York : Verso .

Kerr, Dunlop, Harbison and Myers
1960 Industrialism and Industrial Man . England: Penguin Books

Kiva, Alexi
1989 Developing Countries, Socialism, Capitalism. In International Affairs
NO . 3 : 54 -63 .

Kohler, Heinz

1982 Scarcity, Choice And Optimizing In
Intermediate Micro-economic Theory
And Applications . USA: Oceana Publishers .

Kraus, Jon
1988 The Political Economy Of Trade Union -
state Relations In Radical and
Populist Regimes in Africa in <u>Labour and Unions
In Asia and Africa</u> edited by Roger Southall,
Basingstoke: Macmillan .

Krueger, Anne
1990 Perspectives On Trade and Development.
London: Harvester Wheatsheaf

Larrain, Jorge
1989 Theories Of Development : Capitalism ,
Colonialism and Dependency . Polity Press .

Li, Carmen & Pradhan, Mahmood
1990 Inflation , Financial Liberalization and
Bankruptcies in Argentina. In
<u>International Finance and The Less Developed
Countries,</u> editor Kate
Phylaktis & Mahmood Pradhan. London :
Macmillan.

Lindenfed , F and Rothschild-Whitt , J editors
1982 Workplace Democracy And Social Change.
Boston : Sargent Publishers Inc .

Maddison, Angus
1989 The World Economy In The 20th Century .
OECD: Development centre

Marglin, Stephen
1984 Knowledge And Power. In <u>Firms, Organizations and Labour Approaches To The Economics Of Work Organization</u> edited by Stephen, F. London & Basingstoke: Macmillan

Marx , Karl & Engels F
1970 Manifesto of the Communist Party

Marx, Karl
1974 Capital Vol. I London: Lawerence & Wishart

Moreau, Jacques
1992 An institution Essential for the construction of Europe in The Economic and Special Committee of The European Communities brochure Brussels :ECOSEUR.

Muchie, Mamo & Zon, Hans van
1989 Soviet Foreign Policy Under Gorbachev and Revolution in the Third

This acknowledgment remembers my professors and friends at the Institute of Social Studies. I reproduced it from the thesis to show that I still feel indebted.

ACKNOWLEDGMENT

I am especially indebted to my first supervisor Professor E. Ramaswamy who guided me in my endeavor to come up with a development theory of my own. I am also grateful to my second supervisor Dr Paschal Mihyo, and for Dr. Rachel Kurian for their' critical comments which were very helpful to improving the paper. This does not at all mean they share my views.

I am also indebted to the staff members of the L&D Programme (ISS, the Hague) who have enriched my views in development studies. Professor Henk Thomas, as he was enlightening in his lectures, his private concern during the May crises in my country was of paramount contribution for the completion of the paper on time. Mr Freck Schipohrst's intellectual challenges were invaluable guide to my purpose . Professor Harrod's novel ideas on labour relations have fuelled my interest in the same direction Mrs. Marianne the secretary, was also helpful in many ways. May I not fail them in their expectations.

Thanks is also due to all my Ethiopian friends at ISS and in the Netherlands, with whom I had lively discussions in "The Butterfly" raising many issues on development which were motivating in their own ways.

Last, but not least my gratitude goes respectively, to my country, Ethiopia. and my organization, The Office Of The Wage Board, who sent me to ISS to further my studies and the EEC which covered my fellowship.

www.ingramcontent.com/pod-product-compliance
Lightning Source LLC
Chambersburg PA
CBHW051214170526
45166CB00005B/1894